D1461257

Homecoming

An bealach 'na bhaile

(Photo by Rachel Brown)

Cathal Ó Searcaigh, poet and playwright, lives on a small hill farm at the foot of his beloved Mount Errigal in Co. Donegal. He is the author of three acclaimed volumes of verses, the most represenTive being *Suibhne: Rogha Dánta* (Coiscéim 1988). *Ag Tnúth leis an tSolas*, his fourth collection is expected from Cló Iar-Chonnachta during 1993. His many quirky, irreverent plays include *Mairimid leis na Mistéirí* and *Tá an Tóin ag Titim as an tSaol*. Twice the recipient of Arts Council bursaries in literature he has also held a number of Poet-in-Residence positions. Firmly established as a popular and persuasive performer of poetry he has travelled extensively both at home and abroad giving readings of his work. A selection of his poetry is available on cassette, *An Bealach 'na Bhaile*, isued by Cló Iar-Chonnachta in 1991. He is currently writer-in-residence at the University of Ulster at Coleraine and Queens University, Belfast.

Homecoming

An bealach 'na bhaile

Selected Poems / Rogha Dánta
Cathal Ó Searcaigh

arna chur in eagar ag / edited by

Gabriel Fitzmaurice

réamhrá le / introduction by

Lillis Ó Laoire

Cló Iar-Chonnachta, Indreabhán, Conamara, Éire.

Homecoming/An bealach 'na bhaile
is first published in 1993 by
Cló Iar-Chonnachta Teo., Indreabhán, Conamara, Éire.
Fón: 091-593307. Fax: 091-593362
Second Edition 1993
Third Edition 1995
Fourth Edition 1997
Fifth Edition 2000
Sixth Edition 2004

Cló Iar-Chonnachta receives financial assistance
from The Arts Council (An Chomhairle Ealaíon)

Fuair an t-aistritheoir cabhair airgid ó
Scéim Dleachta Údair na Comhairle Ealaíon.

Cover Painting: "Errigal" by
Caroline Price.
Cover Design: Johan Hofsteenge
Design: Seosaimhín Ní Chonghaile
Deirdre Ní Thuathail
Micheál Ó Conghaile,
Printed and bound in Ireland by
Clódóirí Lurgan Teo., Indreabhán.
Fón: 091-593251/593157 Faics: 091-593159

Acknowledgements

Cló Iar-Chonnachta wish to acknowledge the publishers / editors of the following publications in which the original poems and some translations appeared:

Súile Shuibhne and *Suibhne; An Fhilíocht Chomhaimseartha 1975-1985; Filíocht Uladh 1960-85; Coiscéim na hAoise Seo;* (all from Coiscéim) *The Bright Wave: An Tonn Gheal* (Raven Arts Press), *An Crann faoi Bhláth: The Flowering Tree* (Wolfhound Press), *The Great Book of Ireland; The Field Day Anthology of Irish Literature; Krino; Innti; Salmon; Comhar; An tUltach; die horen,* (Germany). Thanks also to Dr. Peter Kavanagh and The Goldsmith Press Ltd., for the use of one of Patrick Kavanagh's poems from *The Complete Poems* in the Introduction.

Grateful acknowledgement is also made to RTÉ Radio and Television; to Raidió na Gaeltachta and to BBC Radio Ulster for broadcasting some of these poems.

The author wishes to express his sincerest gratitude to all his translators and also to the following who were always generous with their support, their advice and their encouragement in literary matters: Ciaran Carty; Caoimhín Mac Giolla Léith; Pádraig Ó Snodaigh; Douglas Sealy; Caitríona Ní Ghallchóir; Séamus Mac Giolla Chomhaill; Angela Carter; Máirín Seoighe; Máirín Nic Eoin; Alan Titley; Ferdia Mac Anfhailigh; Richard and Sandra; Diarmaid Ó Doibhlin; Micheál Ó Máirtín; Ann Craig; Michael Davitt; Seán Ó Tuama; Micheál Mac A' Bhaird; Nuala Ní Dhomhnaill; Vona and Des Lynn; Máire Mhac an tSaoi; Philip O Leary; Gearóid Denvir; Gearóid Stockman; Eoghan Ó hAnluain; Ciarán Ó Coigligh; Theo Dorgan; Liam Ó Muirthile; Lar Cassidy; Frank Harvey; Valerie Lynch; Máire Nic Suibhne; Liam Ó Cuinneagáin; Murray Learmont; Michael Ferry; Máirín Ní Dhubhchoin; Noel Ó Gallchóir; Maitiú Ó Murchú; Peigí Rose; Tom Walsh; Máire Nic Niallais; Deirdre Davitt; Denise Marshall; Séamus Mac Annaidh; Brian Mullins; Louis de Paor; Proinsias Ní Dhorchaí; Proinsias Ó Drisceoil; Liam Mac Cóil; Tadhg Mac Dhonnagáin; Liam Desmond and especially Rachel Brown; Jarleth Donnelly; Lillis Ó Laoire; Heather Allen; Gréagóir Ó Dúill and the irreplaceable Gabriel Rosenstock.

for Micheál Ó Searcaigh
my father
for his graciousness and his Poetry:
for Traolach Ó Fionnáin
our enterprising
Arts Officer in Co. Donegal, for his indefatigable
promotion of the Arts:

An Clár / Contents

Cuid / Part I

Cuid / Part II

Cuid / Part III

Cuid / Part IV

Cuid / Part V

Cathal Ó Searcaigh is one of a number of Irish poets who have unabashedly opened up to the world of the spirit, to the inner world where one is neither male nor female, Catholic nor Protestant, Hindu nor Buddhist; where the laws, if laws there be, of poetic and aesthetic propriety do not obtain. It is useless for the pedant to protest, the cleric to complain, the feminist to find fault, the city to censure — his is a free spirit that goes its own way with a good wish to all.

It would be easy for any, or all, of the above to accuse Ó Searcaigh of transgression, but that would be to miss the point. Ó Searcaigh is not an inept poet, irreligious, sexist nor culchie. These four areas are central to a poetic that is, in my reading, sensual and sensuous, a hymn to the human body as incarnation of the soul. He writes as much as a woman as as a man — not as androgyne but as one in whom the *yin* and *yang* of Chinese dualistic philosophy find expression, complementing each other and informing not only his poetry but his life. Like many before him, not all of them hippies, dope freaks or persons disaffected with society and/or disenchanted with themselves, Ó Searcaigh has turned to the east and eastern philosophy and religion to complement his Catholic upbringing. In so doing, he frees himself from the puritanism of Irish Catholicism and gains a celebratory vision which informs his poetry, placing him beyond the strictures of dogma where he comes to terms personally with the divine. I do not expect the cynical modern sensibility, crippled by angst and nausea, to make this leap with Ó Searcaigh into the light. But it might at least allow him his jump, even if all leaps, inevitably, end up back on the ground. It is the leap that matters — the leap and the mind it creates.

He would appear to be a sitting duck for feminist censure. And not without reason. Does he *compromise women with all his talk of sex and his own pleasure?* Ultimately I think not. He seems to me to be very naively, for which read "simply and honestly", celebrating the creative act, poetic as well as sexual. He can hardly be blamed for its concomitant pleasure. Indeed, the centrality of women to him is revealed in *Súile Shuibhne* in which he states: "B'ise mo mhaoinín, b'ise mo Ghort a' Choirce" ("She was my darling, she was my *Gort a' Choirce*" — i.e. his home place). This is the central image, I feel, in the whole book. Place becomes person, significantly a woman. The *yin* is uppermost. He is a poet in exile (in the city, away from home, in the English language, in formal religion) and the thrust (the *yang*) of his poetry is to return to fertile ground, the sanctuary where he can be whole and fruitful. This he achieves in a poetry that is mellifluous and melodic, sensuous and sensual.

Eventually, like many artists, he achieves a sense of being at home in exile:

> "Now I pick up *Mín 'a Leá* and Mayfair
> On the same mad miraculous
> Frequency in my mind
> In this buzz I feel in Berkeley Square;
> While I discover myself with a positiveness
> I haven't already felt
> My own vibe, my own rhythm
> The exciting rhythm of life increasing and buzzing
> In the arteries that are my words.
>
> Like a flock of sheep being driven to the mountain
> The traffic is bleating
> Uneasily on the roads
> From Park Lane to Piccadilly
> And in all directions
> The offices.... grey green city mountains
> Sun themselves and rejoice in the May sunshine,
> For the first time I feel at home abroad."

Home is where the word is.

He is not afraid of using certain words, words that tend to annoy the modern English-language reviewer. Words like "animated", "wholesome", "pure", "God", "heaven", "chalice", "desire" come naturally to him and invite us to a world where language is free of inhibition returning to its true function: to convey meaning, shades of meaning and attitude as clearly or as obliquely as its terms and context allow. Ó Searcaigh, then, with the sensitivity of a poet and the sensibility of a child ("Whosoever shall not receive the Kingdom of God as a little child, he shall not enter therein"), invites us to join him on his journey, echoing Jack Kerouac's, which "zigzags all over creation... Ain't nowhere else it can go". Like any worthwhile journey, it is an internal journey, a personal quest. A mystical journey that doesn't deal in easy mysticism. A journey that sets out from Gort a' Choirce, his physical, emotional and spiritual home, a journey that ends as it begins in the full knowledge that in *the age of want... there will have to be a going back to the sources*".

Gabriel Fitzmaurice
Moyvane, Co. Kerry.
29 January 1992

Introduction: A Yellow Spot on the Snow

Is grá geal mo chroí thú
A Thír Chonaill a stór,
I do luí mar bheadh seoid ghlas
San fharraige mhór.

You are my truelove
Tír Chonaill my darling
Lying like a green jewel
In the great ocean.

The above sentimental song composed during the nationalist and cultural revival around the turn of the century speaks of Donegal almost as if it were an island and seems almost prophetic in hindsight, since the partition which came with self-determination served to cut Donegal off to a large extent from its natural hinterland. It is joined to the rest of the republic only by a narrow band of land in the extreme south of the county. Therefore Donegal is in many senses an island, isolated and distinct with its own unique mindcast. It is ironic that, although part of what is known in current parlance as the "south", it is the northernmost of any of Ireland's thirty two counties. The continuing violence in Northern Ireland discourages many potential visitors, so that Donegal has not as yet fully succumbed to the naked commercialism of more accessible southern regions.

Donegal, *Dún na nGall,* means the Fort of the Foreigners. Originally the name only applied to Donegal Castle in the south of the county but it has come to be used in both languages for the whole region. *Tír Chonaill* — Land of Conall — which the song celebrates is a much older name and properly used excludes *Inis Eoghain*, the peninsula of Eoghan, in the north east. Both Conall and Eoghan were sons of Niall Naoi-Ghiallach, High King of Ireland in the early fifth century and ancestor of the Uí Néill, a dynasty which controlled the succession to the High Kingship for five hundred years. Most of the aristocratic families of Gaelic Ulster claimed descent from him in former times. *Tír Eoghain — Land of Eoghan* — is also named for this Eoghan. Conall Gulban is known as the ancestor of *Cinéal Conaill*, the interrelated Donegal tribes of whom the O'Donnells became the most powerful and the best known. They were traditional hereditary chieftains of Donegal until the seventeenth century when the native order finally ceased to exist independently of English rule. In the middle ages Donegal maintained links with the wider Gaelic world both in the rest of Ireland and in the Lordship of the Isles in Scotland. There was a lot of movement back and forth at this time. The Scottish Gaels often provided mercenary fighting men, known as *Gallóglaigh* — Gallowglasses — for Irish leaders in time of war. Many of these settled in Donegal afterwards, a fact which the surnames of the area bear out. The origin of the Mac Sweeneys is well documented and MacPháidín and Mac Íomhair are but two other examples of local surnames which are also found in the Scottish Highlands. There was also intermarriage between the aristocratic families of Ulster and Scotland. The formidable Inghean Dubh, for example, a very ambitious character and the mother of Red Hugh O'Donnell was a Mac Donald from Islay and was known in her own day as "great bringer in of Scots."

The variety of Irish spoken in Donegal forms part of a linguistic continuum which stretches from Lewis in the north to Cape Clear in the south. Donegal Irish has many similarities to Gàidhlig. These were formerly attributed to the movements which have just been referred to, but now some scholars take the view that they are indigenous and not due

14

to any overt Scottish influence. Whatever their origin, these affinities render Donegal Irish different in many respects from the Irish spoken further south. This, together with Donegal's marginal location, causes many southern speakers to say that they cannot understand the dialect. Recently indeed, a row erupted when some southern teachers objected to the dialect being included in listening comprehension tests set by the Department of Education. Such prejudice, though commoner than might be wished, is not general. Although most competent speakers not unnaturally prefer their own dialect, they view the difference as interesting and exciting and do not feel threatened by it.

Donegal is a place of many contrasts. The fertile district of east Donegal is markedly different to the wilder and more barren west. The people of the west generally refer to this region as *An Lagán*. Much of the western area is designated as Gaeltacht or Irish-speaking although casual visitors may be disappointed in many districts if they expect to hear Irish spoken as the vernacular. Most of the area marked on the map will contain native Irish speakers but in many places English has become the usual everyday language. Irish is maintained in these as a second, lesser-used language. Linguistic competence generally decreases among the younger people in such communities. Their main contact with Irish will usually come from school and some may later choose to increase their fluency by joining a youth club or a drama group. The language becomes an occasional medium for them and they do not readily perceive it as a real language. Some however do make that transition and also become actively committed to arresting the further marginalisation of Irish in their localities.

It is believed that before the collapse of the Gaelic order, the western region of Donegal was very sparsely populated, although remains of human habitation survive the Mesolithic era. In 1609, during the Plantation of Ulster, the more fertile areas of the province were granted to English and lowland Scots and the Irish were allocated to the poorer, more mountainy land. It was at this time that many people moved into west Donegal. Here they lived just as they had always lived, self-sufficient

15

and independent, with little interference from the state. They worked the land and created the landscape to which Ó Searcaigh is so attached:

Here I feel permanence
as I look at the territory of my people
round the foot of Errigal
where they've settled
for more than three hundred years
on the grassy mountain pastures...
Above and below, I see the holdings
farmed from the mouth of wilderness.
This is the poem-book of my people,
the manuscript they toiled at
with the ink of their sweat.

Here at Caiseal na gCorr Station / Anseo ag Stáisiún Chaiseal na gCorr

Things continued in this manner until around the time of the Famine when the people began gradually to be drawn into a consumer economy. Shops were opened and the need for cash prompted many parents to send their children to work on the large farms in the *Lagán* district. The contract was usually for six months, the labour extremely hard and the wages a pittance. This practice continued until about fifty years ago. It was quite normal for children as young as nine years to go to the *Lagán* and they usually spent about five or six seasons on the *Lagán* before going further afield to the large farms and industrial cities of Scotland. The *Lagán* was considered child's work and the wages were better across the North Channel. The men began to go to Scotland around the same time and in doing so began a pattern which survived until the early nineteen sixties. They would often spend the better part of the year in Scotland working on the farms, coming home only in spring to help their women till their own small patch of ground. This life is well documented

16

in the regional literature, for example by Micí Mac Gabhann in *Rotha Mór an tSaoil* (translated as *The Hard Road to Klondyke*). Cathal's parents, Mickey Sharkey and Agnes Roarty, lived this life. Mickey's passport for the war years gives "migratory labourer" as his occupation. Cathal has celebrated his mother's experiences in his adaptation of Derick Thomson's *Clann Nighean na Scadan; Cailíní na Scadán/The Herring Girls*:

It was, history's confused mess which had left them abroad
slaves to the herring curers, to the short-arsed upstarts
in the towns of British Ports
from Lerwick in Shetland down to Yarmouth in England.
Well-seasoned was their prize, by God,
from the unceasing filling of the barrels
the sea wind sharp on their skin
and a burden of poverty
in their coffers
and but for their laughter
you would think that their hearts were broken.

In the nineteen fifties and sixties many young couples chose to remain abroad and some settled in Glasgow where there is a vigorous Donegal community to this day. Emigration reached its peak during these decades but slowed to a trickle in the seventies as better opportunities became available at home. Such emigration as there was then was more a matter of choice than of necessity. In the eighties emigration accelerated again, though it was not to Scotland that this generation looked but to south-eastern Britain, the cities of the United States and Australia. Although they were better educated than any of their predecessors, this did not decrease their sense of isolation in their new environment. Perhaps their education indeed heightened their awareness of their position and made

17

them more critical of the successive governments who failed to provide an alternative. By the nineties the Thatcherite boom had ended in recession and many of the emigrants have returned home, believing it preferable to live on the dole in a rural environment than in a foreign city:

To-morrow I travel on to a haven
Beyond the pitch and brawl of the seas:
The flats round here are a run-down graveyard
Where my young self walks like a nameless zombie.

Triall/Will Travel

Emigration then for the last hundred and fifty years has been a fact of life for the people of Donegal and has left its mark on their personality. The dream is to go away and to return a success and many achieve a version of this dream. More do not and they deal with it in different ways. In an attempt to preserve the illusion of success some never come back. Others return, not having succeeded abroad and became involved once again in the life of their home place. Their homecoming and resumption of their old lives is perhaps the most difficult decision. The Scottish writer Iain Crichton Smith himself from a rural, Gàidhlig speaking background, accurately describes the dilemma: "To return home is not simply to return home, it is to return to a community, for one's gains and losses to be assessed. The community is the ultimate critic, not easily taken in, with its own system of checks and balances." There are those who settle in the cities, marry, and bring up their families there. Their isolation is to a large extent replaced by an accommodation to the values of their chosen environment. They become cultural amphibians, functioning equally well at home and abroad, although this facility is not without its tensions and contradictions. Again Smith's insight into the matter is invaluable: "When I left the village community in order to attend the secondary school in Stornoway I felt as if I was abandoning the community

18

There was a subtle alteration to me in the attitude of my contemporaries who were not taking the road of education but would work on the land or on the fishing boats. Even now when I meet members of the community who have stayed at home there is a slight constraint in our relationship, there is a human distance. I have made the choice, I have forsaken the community in order to individualise myself."

This statement is reminiscent of one made by Seosamh Mac Grianna in *Mo Bhealach Féin*: "*Tá babhún dímheasa idir an té a théid chun coláiste agus an té nach dtéid.*" 'A wall of contempt stands between the one who is educated and the one who is not.' In a striking simile Smith compares the community to a spider's web, where if one part is pulled the remainder trembles. In such a society everyone is part of the whole and no one person takes precedence over the rest. The community has its strengths in its concern for all its members and the structures which enable people to give practical expression to that concern. It has its own unwritten rules beyond which no one may go without risking censure. Smith discusses the concept of *cliù* which he translates as moral reputation or standing. This reputation once lost cannot be regained. The community judgement lasts until the fourth generation and beyond. In fact this same word, *cliú,* is used to express the same idea in Donegal. It is significant in this context that the American ethnographer Henry Glassie has pointed out that lying, theft and murder are classed as crimes of equal gravity. Indeed he infers that stealing is feared almost more than murder, since it is the clearest instance of an attack by one member of the community on another who is innocent. Such attacks deeply offend the delicate balance necessary for its proper functioning. The desire to keep the machinery of the community smoothly running also accounts for the dislike of individualism. In more recent years the community has changed. Constant exposure to television and the aggressive consumerism promoted by advertising have had their effects. People nowadays lock their doors since crime is no longer unheard of and it is often perpetrated by members of the local community. Ó Searcaigh marks the change in *An Tobar/The Well*:

But this long time, piped water from distant hills
sneaks into every kitchen
on both sides of the glen;
mawkish, without sparkle,
zestless as slops
and among my people
the springwell is being forgotten.

A word is necessary on Donegal's literary tradition which dates back to Bardic times when the O'Donnells and other aristocratic families maintained a professional class which included poets, historians and lawyers. Indeed one sixteenth century chief, Mánas Ó Domhnaill, has achieved lasting fame as a scholar and poet. At his castle in Lifford in 1542 he compiled the famous biography of his kinsman St Colm Cille. In the seventeenth century the patronage upon which the professional classes depended gradually ceased as the Gaelic aristocracy either emigrated or adopted English ways and customs. The custody of the native learning then passed to the ordinary people who, with succeeding generations became more remote from the bardic heritage. There was never a strong manuscript tradition of literary transmission here, unlike areas such as Munster and south-east Ulster where scribal activity continued well into the second half of the nineteenth century. The literature and culture of the people was transmitted by oral means for over three centuries. Inspired by the romantic movement and the growth of cultural nationalism which accompanied it, the upper classes found that the unlettered peasants, as they perceived them, possessed a heritage of their own which had hitherto remained unnoticed. Enthusiasts began to collect this material which they believed was in danger of imminent loss, and in 1927 the Irish Folklore Commission was established to systematically record this disappearing tradition. The Donegal man most associated with this collection is Seán Ó hEochaidh, a native of *Teileann,* who spent fifty years engaged in this work. The results of his vast labour are stored in the archive of the Department of Irish Folklore at University College Dublin.

Oral literature takes many forms. In the past storytelling and singing were regarded as the highest artistic expressions of it. The *scéalaí* was a specialist whose province was the telling of the old stories. A special narrative style characterises these tales and great skill was required to tell them properly. The practitioners were generally older men. *Seanchas* was another distinct branch of learning, a term which can best be translated as local knowledge. This term was used in the days of the Gaelic aristocracy to define history. Seán Ó hEochaidh's main informant for the *Gort a' Choirce* area was Niall Ó Dubhthaigh, from whom he recorded over four and a half thousand manuscript pages of detailed knowledge on every aspect of local life. The songs belonged more generally to the community and the singing of them was an important part of any social gathering. This branch of culture also had its specialists who could be counted upon to remember rarer items of the community repertoire. There were of course the exceptional individuals who excelled at all three branches of traditional learning. Anna Nic a'Luain from *Na Cruacha Gorma* — the Bluestacks — springs immediately to mind. She gave the Folklore Commission fifty long stories, the texts of 250 songs and numerous items of *seanchas*. She was unable to speak English. Seán Ó hEochaidh compared her to a spring well during a long summer drought: every evening the well would be empty and on returning the next morning it was found replenished with clear life-giving liquid.

It is fashionable nowadays to point out that Ireland has been a bilingual society since the middle ages. This reminder is issued to counter the "monolithic Gaelic model" which nationalists put forward during the earlier part of this century. English was spoken in Ireland during the middle ages but it was certainly restricted to the areas outside Gaelic control. The important point is not the existence of the language but its relationship with the dominant Irish language. The speaking of English in those days was quite naturally seen as a mark of education and an accomplishment to be enjoyed in much the same way as a continental language is seen today. The relationship was one of equality and there was certainly no thought at this time of replacing the native language with the other. This changed with the complete subjugation of Gaelic culture during the seventeenth century. The relationship of the languages changed. Irish was deprived of any official status and English became the only language of administration and law. The aristocracy became an English-speaking class. Irish was seen as backward, a mark of ignorance and poverty, and all who wished to advance under the new régime made the English language their medium of communication. This change was gradual but steady until after the Famine when it accelerated dramatically. English was established in Donegal during the early seventeenth century but Irish continued to maintain itself strongly side by side with it until about the eighteen fifties or sixties. Many factors contributed to the shift, some of which I have already mentioned. As the people became increasingly bilingual they began to assimilate the songs of the new language. Child ballads such as *Barbara Allen* and *John Barbour* became part of the repertoire as did songs like *A Lady Walked in her Father's Garden*. Ballad sheets hawked at fairs by professional singers contributed many more new songs to the repertoire. Some of the Gaelic songs acquired English equivalents to their verses:

Tá mo chleamhnas a dhéanamh inniu agus inné
Is ní mó ná go dtaitníonn an bhean adaí liom féin
Ach fuígfidh mé mo dhiaidh í is rachaidh mé leat féin
Fá bhruach na coilleadh craobhaí.

My match is a-making since ere last night
It isn't with the girl that I love the best;
I'll leave her behind me and go along with you
Down by the banks of the ocean.

Many of the poets resolved to try their hand at composition in the new language with surprisingly successful results at times:

To see my darling on a summer's morning
When Flora's fragrance bedecked the lawn,
Her neat deportment and manners courteous
Around her sporting the lamb and fawn.
On high I ponder where'er I wander
And still grow fonder sweet maid of thee;
Of your matchless charms I am enamoured:
"O Moorlough Mary won't you come away."

The rhyming scheme here is a tell tale sign that that the poet knew Irish and was consciously imitating Gaelic models. Devotional anthems to place, combined with an emigration theme, abounded:

Attention pay my countrymen and hear my native news
Although my song is sorrowful I hope you'll me excuse
I left my peaceful residence a foreign land to see
And I bade farewell to Donegal, likewise to Glenswilly.

These songs proved immensely popular and remain so to this day. It is said that people in the past sang these songs in English without being fluent in the language themselves. They were sung in the same style as the Irish language songs, often to Gaelic airs. Because of the relationship of the two languages the songs in English often served to severely undermine the Gaelic songs. In many Gaeltacht areas the song repertoire

23

gradually became mainly English, even in areas where Irish was dominant. A passage from an Irish-language novel serves to illustrate one of the reasons for it. This scene is set in Scotland among some some migratory workers:

"You ought to ask Donnchadh Ó Leadhain to sing a song," said Róise. "He has a lovely voice. Don't you remember him the other night."
"He has a fine voice without a doubt," said Seán 'Ac Conaglaigh's daughter. "Unfortunately he has only Irish songs. He was reared by his grandmother. He hasn't one single song in English. Of course he'd sing us an Irish song, and a dozen of them, if he were asked. But you'd never know that some of the Scots weren't eavesdropping on us somewhere. He shamed us one night last year. He sang 'Mal Dubh a' Ghleanna' while there were a few Scots with us. But there's a man who has plenty of songs and a fairly good voice — Éamonn Ó Dochartaigh. I must ask our Mící to ask him to sing."
"Edward Doherty will now oblige the company with a song."

Irish became so undermined that in many cases even the language of song making became English in staunchly Irish-speaking areas. Indeed many of the writers of the Irish revival, Cathal Ó Searcaigh among them, actually attempted composition in English before turning to their native language. The language revival brought a renewal of interest in the Irish-language songs. As they saw these urban enthusiasts returning year after year, attempting to acquire the very things thought so unfashionable by themselves, many gained an appreciation of, and insight into, the culture that they cherished but had come to regard as an anachronistic hindrance to progess. This effected something of a reversal of the shift among some of the people. In fact the awareness of what was being lost prompted a reaction among many so that in the last two generations singers have emerged who cultivated a predominantly Irish language repertoire. The great authority on all aspects of the folk tradition of his native *Rinn na Feirste,* Aodh Ó Duibheannaigh is known to have had very few English language songs in his active repertoire. Caitlín Ní Dhomhnaill, also a *Rinn na Feirste* singer, but of a younger generation, also sings almost exclusively in Irish. Another singer, from Tory Island, once remarked to me that he preferred singing in Irish because he had a mastery in it which he did not feel in English. The revival of interest stimulated new compositions in Irish. Many of these show the influence of the song making tradition in English in both theme and form. The intricate assonantal patterns, together with many of the formulaic conventions of older Gaelic verse are absent and end rhyme predominates. One such song, the enduringly popular *Cnoc A' Diaraigh,* was made by a relative of Cathal's. Ciarán Carson, in his introduction to Rachel Giese's *The Donegal Pictures,* has commented that the photographs represent a macaronic or mixed landscape. The oral culture also reflects the alternation of Irish and English, what Carson calls the debate between them.

This complex bilingual culture has influenced many Irish writers, those of Donegal being no exception. The work of Patrick Magill, Seamus Mac Manus, Peadar O'Donnell, Patrick McGinley, Frank McGuinness, and Matthew Sweeney testifies to a debt to the traditions of their communities. Nowhere is this more evident than in the dramas of Brian Friel, who again and again returns to Donegal for the settings of his plays. The resonances have to a great extent maintained themselves in the new language. Largely because of the nationalist and cultural revival at the turn of the century, there are also some Donegal writers whose chosen medium was the Irish language. The two most talented members of this group were brothers, descended on their mother's side from the "Filí gan Iomrá", the unsung poets of Rinn na Feirste, whose greatest literary achievement, *An Chéad Mháirt de Fhómhar,* is still an integral feature of Rinn na Feirste identity. This is the passionate elegy of Séamas Ó Domhnaill for his drowned son Pádraig:

The first Tuesday of autumn my story was sad and weary
A capable, courageous hand preceding me on the deathbed,
On the Rock of Tears I suppose I lost my sight
And until I am lain beneath the sod I will never recover since you are gone.

My curse forever on the edge of this shore below
It has left your People depressed and has turned my heart to black coal,
Laying you to rest in your grave has left me without strength
Bereft of courage and reason, a poor wretch tossed by the wind.

As with so many Irish songs, it is not complete without a knowledge of the accompanying narrative where for example, it emerges that the father probably regarded himself as partly responsible for the tragedy. Both Séamas and Seosamh Mac Grianna belonged to an exceptional family of storytellers and poets and have made invaluable contributions to the development of modern Irish literature in the twentieth century. Séamas, the older and more traditional of the two, is among the great stylists of Irish language prose. He based his writing on the oral tradition and produced novels and stories which have a unique polish and elegance. He is often criticised for having kept too close to traditional storytelling models and for consequent weaknesses of plot and characterisation. Nevertheless his masterful handling of language assures him an undisputed place among the writers of the Irish literary renaissance. His brother Seosamh has an even stronger position in this regard. Feeling the constraints of his brother's staunch traditionalism, he broke away from that particular mould and tried to develop a dynamic, modern, literary medium from the same material his brother had used to forge his own mode of expression. He experimented with form, transforming the tried and tested Gaeltacht biography into the subversive classic *Mo Bhealach Féin*, thereby taking Irish prose from the Homeric and placing it in the post-modern era in the space of a few years. He was a tortured and restless spirit and his health failed him, ending his writing career abruptly

in his mid-thirties. Niall Ó Dónaill, another Rosses writer, deserves
mention in the development of Donegal writing. Although his output
was small, *Na Glúnta Rosannacha,* a study of the Rosses from the earliest
period to modern times, shows a writer of discipline and character
exercising to the full the resources available in his native language. Fionn
Mac Cumhaill and Ó Searcaigh's own kinsman, Tadhg Ó Rabhartaigh,
number among the other writers in this school.

Cathal Ó Searcaigh then, is not a writer functioning in a void, but
one with a highly developed and varied tradition behind him. Ó
Searcaigh's closest literary antecedent is perhaps Seosamh Mac Grianna,
also the product of an essentially oral community, and he freely
acknowledges the influence of the oral literature in the Irish language
upon him. The lyric song poetry of the eighteenth and nineteenth
centuries, with its intricate vowel rhyming and its sinuous grace, provide
him with possibilities for experimenting with theme and form. The
passionate, intense simplicity of the love songs continues to inspire and
delight him. Here is a translation of one of his favourites:

I am awake since the moon rose last night,
Ceaselessly lighting the fire and ever tending it,
The people of the house are asleep and I am alone,
The cocks are crowing and the world asleep but me.

My pure delight is your mouth, your brow, your cheek,
Your sparkling, blue eye for which I forsook pleasure and fun,
With longing for you I cannot see the road which I walk,
And my dearest friend, the mountains stand between me and you.

People of education say that love is a miserable disease,
I never admitted it until it had tortured the heart inside me,
A sharp sore pain, alas I did not avoid it,
It has pierced my heart a hundredfold with its darts.

27

I met a woman of the sí down at the fort at the ford's mouth,
And asked her whether there was a key to unlock this love,
She answered in a low voice with words both calm and serene,
When it goes to the heart it never again is released.

The bare translation gives an idea of the original, even without its word-music and its melody, which in the hands of a skilled traditional singer becomes a poignant statement of lost love, speaking directly from the heart. This song is a well known standard in the living repertoire of Donegal singers. The precedents set by these songs are an important resource for Ó Searcaigh, enabling him to explore this area of his emotional life in a truly personal fashion. *Ceann Dubh Dílis/My Blackhaired Love* is perhaps the most obvious example of such exploration. From a lyric of the same name, Cathal adapts the song to his own experience, dealing with homosexual love, a theme which has until now seldom appeared in Irish language literature:

My blackhaired love, my dear, dear, dear,
Our kiss re-opens Christ's wounds here:
But close your mouth, don't spread the word:
We offend the Gospels with our love.

You plague the local belles, my sweet,
They attempt to coax you with deceit
But you'd prefer my lonely kiss,
You hugging me to bring to bliss.

Love was not the only concern of the eighteenth century poets. Their own poetic reputations were often uppermost in their minds as when Eoghan Mac Niallais of Ard A' Ratha and Séamas Ó Doraidheáin of Cill Charthaigh competed to find out who was the better poet. Each made songs in praise of mountains in their own areas, Eoghan praising *An*

28

Mhaoineach and Séamas choosing the majestic *Sliabh Liag* for his subject. Significantly the verses were set to the same tune as it would have been inconceivable to compose a poem without music. Eoghan's inspiration petered out after only four verses and his composition was soundly beaten by Séamas' tour de force of nine eight-line stanzas. Here are a few by way of illustration:

Great beautiful Sliabh Liag on which grows long grass
With yellow honey flowing like dew on the slopes of its passes
Which has excelled every hill even as far as Tara
To Nephin Mac Amhlaidh to Antrim and to the Boyne.
The fairs there are full of pleasure, woods filled with joy
And slender ships of the Sí as they set sail
The coaches of princes approach by roads
There is an abundance of butter and sweet cow's milk .

This is the peaked fresh hill with its orchards and apples
The bees collecting nectar and its clusters of ripe nuts
There is no fruit which does not grow on the heather there
And there is a sweet fragrance pervading to the very top.
Barley in stacks, wheat in sheaves
Yellow cheese, cream and soft rushes growing
Eternal summer with the calling of cuckoos and blackbirds
And the sleek steer advancing to the top of the pass.

At the foot of Áine's hillock there is a bright court and parlour
Limewhite walls and chessmen ready for play
And to the great hostels of the mountain hundreds proceed
To weddings and feasts and other such events from all parts,
There is a host of richly dressed Greek women there with curling tresses
Being entertained by harp and pipe music
And how sweet to me is the cuckoo singing in solitude
From the top of a rush clump, or at the upper end of For Aoidh.

The superb hyperbole of this song, with its references to mythology and its emphasis on fertility and natural abundance, comes directly from medieval tradition, although it is thought to have been composed after 1798. In modern day terms it is perhaps difficult to accept the sincerity of *Sliabh Liag*, but it must be remembered that the poet in Gaelic Ireland was a feared and revered person. Francis John Byrne has correctly suggested that "The poetic formula... of the *fili* was by its very nature a truth. Such at least seems to have been the dogma which lingered in the sub-conscious of the Christian Irish until modern times, and which redeemed the flattery of bardic panegyrics." It is obvious that this idea underlies *Sliabh Liag* and it is also important to remember that the *filíocht* in Irish was not synonymous with composition in English. The poetry of Cathal Ó Searcaigh belongs to this archaic tradition while at the same time it is intensely and uncompromisingly modern. His utterances also aim to express the truth, even though his perceptions differ greatly from the traditional concepts.

Cathal Ó Searcaigh has acknowledged another debt, to the people who exercised a formative influence upon him in his early youth. He has been accused of sentimental nostalgia, but this is a misunderstanding of his purpose. Poems such as *Oícheanta Geimhridh/Winter Nights* and *Bean An tSléibhe / Mountain Woman* properly acknowledge the richness that these people gave him although he was not completely aware of its importance at the time. Once, at a poetry recitation competition when *Oícheanta Geimhridh* was recited, a man beside me remarked, "I knew Neddie Eoin well and I never heard him talking of things like that." The wisdom of the old people was there for the taking but not everyone availed of the opportunity:

It's not aging I am, but ripening
and her words fell like seeds into the welcoming earth of my mind.

And when she'd wrap me in her limbs so tightly
I felt the fat, the growth rings of her body.

Now and again I have a Mass said for her
in memory of the fruit she bestowed on me
from the Tree of Knowledge...

The gifts can only be given to the receptive: the seeds do not sprout in the earth of every mind.

Cloch Cheannfhaola, Cloughaneely, where Cathal Ó Searcaigh was born and lives, is situated in the north-west of the county. Together with the neighbouring parishes of *Gaoth Dobhair* and *Na Rosa,* it forms the heartland of the Donegal Gaeltacht. The dramatic outline of *Toraigh* or Tory Island, which Heinrich Wagner described as the last stronghold of Ulster Irish, can be seen on the horizon. The Irish language maintains itself with varying degrees of strength in this region which, although remote, is surprisingly suburban in many respects. The largest population centre is Falcarragh, which now as in the past is the main focus of the community. It has always been an English-speaking town and serves to intensify the constant pressure of anglicisation on the Irish-speaking community. Older people have memories of being ridiculed publicly there for their inability to transact business in English. The situation has changed quite a lot in latter years and the casual visitor might be deceived into believing that the language is widely spoken by the people of the town. Although more families than formerly maintain Irish as their home language in Falcarragh, Irish speaking families, living in local authority housing there, experience great difficulties in transmitting the language to their children. It is in cases such as this that the lack of a language policy at local authority level undermines and makes a mockery of the professed national aim of the restoration of the Irish language. Indeed the placing of Irish speaking families in a predominantly English-speaking housing estate, in an English-speaking

31

village, is rightly viewed by many as an insensitive and linguistically destructive act.

So much bad poetry has been written in defence of the language that any poet must now be wary of writing propaganda. Ó Searcaigh's statement about the language is saved from this by being at once a public condemnation and a statement of intense personal loss. The death of the language is compared to the horror experienced by a child witnessing a pet sheep being devoured alive by hooded crows:

To-day it's my language that's in its throes,
The poets' passion, my mothers' fathers'
Mothers' language, abandoned and trapped
On a fatal ledge that we won't attempt.
She's in agony, I can hear her heave
And gasp and struggle as they arrive,
The beaked and ravenous scavengers
Who are never far. Oh if only anger
Came howling wild out of her grief,
If only she'd bare the teeth of her love
And rout the pack. But she's giving in,
She's quivering badly, my mother's gone
And promises now won't ease the pain.

Caoineadh/Lament

His mother's comfort and security has eased the pain of the first barbarous episode but now, alone, there seems to be no healing balm in store. Irish is more strongly maintained in the rural areas west of *Na Croisbhealaí* — Crossroads — as Falcarragh is also known. The area's second village, *Gort a' Choirce,* which stands at the estuary of the *Gleann Átha* river has not been subject the the rapid changes which have characterised the growth of its larger counterpart. Consequently the

32

language is in a better state there. Although it is true to say that it is the small farmers and fishermen in the outlying areas who display most linguistic loyalty there are many exceptions to this pattern. Many people who are employed in the factories in *Gaoth Dobhair's* industrial estate also live in relatively remote areas, so in dealing with the area we must rid ourselves of any notion of a Celtic Paradise. The society here is complex although this may not be evident at first glance. It is one where some live in the traditional way and others have little contact with their rural environment. Of course many tread a sometimes uneasy path between these two extremes and their contradictory value systems. These values are to some extent symbolised by the two languages, Irish being perceived as more conservative, more old fashioned, upholding parental authority in all matters and generally out of touch with the modern world. English on the other hand seems to hold out the promise of eternal youth, of high status, designer products, limitless freedom and opportunity. This has implications especially for the young who will always want to conform to peer pressure. The postprimary school, located in Falcarragh, seems to support this symbolism. The medium of instruction there has always been English, although some attempts have been made to disguise this fact. Thus the impression of the superiority of English is reinforced at school. It will come as no surprise then, that teenagers favour English more than Irish when amongst themselves. Of course important exceptions exist to this general rule and some display high levels of linguistic loyalty. Cathal himself has obviously felt this division as we can see from his description of Irish in an urban environment:

Clad in old world homespun
She is as gullible as myself
In the city slickness;
As ungainly as a hobnailed stepdancer
In a Russian Ballet.

Mise Charlie An Scibhí/I am Charlie the Scivvy

Cathal Ó Searcaigh is a poet of this place and this landscape. His voice gives vivid expression to his feeling of intimacy with his *Gleann Átha,* the Valley of the Ford. This is not only a geographical location but a country of the imagination which the poet recreates in each poem. As Dante Della Terza has stated in the introduction to the work of Rocco Scotellaro, an Italian poet form Luciana with whom Ó Searcaigh strongly identifies: "His poetry gives us not a realistic topography, but the internal measure of space: an *espace du dedans* which is farther reaching and more telling than any geographic remoteness." The landscape for Ó Searcaigh is at once his long lost lover welcoming him home after years of absence and a sanctuary which gives meaning to his existence and his poetry. Nevertheless the claustrophobia which is part of all small communities emerges from his verse in no uncertain terms and perhaps this serves to temper his celebratory lyricism. One of his functions is the empowerment of the word, his infusion of new energies into everyday clichés which might to others seem beyond redemption as vehicles of poetic expression. Again, speaking of Scotellaro, Della Terza has said that he "was aware that life cannot truly change if words do not free themselves from eroded habits and sclerotic routines." The same may be said of Ó Searcaigh. There is no poem which surprises us more in this respect than *Cor Úr / A Fresh Dimension* where in a juxtaposition of the workaday placenames of the Glen, Ó Searcaigh recreates them as human features. The association has a transforming effect on our perception and liberates us from our conditioned response to our immediate environment.

from Log Dhroim na Gréine to Alt na hUillinne
from Malaidh Rua to Mín na hUchta
below and above, body most beautiful,
every cavity and curve, every sunspot,
every beauty-spot I'd forgotten

since last I was with you.

The problem of transliterating Irish placenames has been a difficult one and most became travesties of their original in the system used by the surveyors of the nineteenth century. This theme, among others, has been dealt with by Brian Friel in *Translations*. The policy adopted by translators in this volume is to leave the placenames in the original. Literal translation is however necessary here for a fuller understanding of the poem. *Log Dhroim na Gréine* becomes the hollow of the sunny ridge. *Droim* is also the ordinary Irish word for back. Similarly *alt* can mean a hillock or stream as well as a joint while *uillinn* is an elbow. *Malaidh* can be a brae or a brow, *ucht* is a slope or the human chest. The idea of the earth goddess as the lover of the king is an archaic and tenacious one in Gaelic poetry so much so as to render it forbidden territory to modern poets in search of an original voice. Ó Searcaigh again transforms this idea into an extremely personal response of the returning emigrant while still retaining the age-old resonances. The personification of place in both its benevolent and malignant aspects pervades his poetry. He is aware of its hold over himself and others. In *Bó Bhradach / A Braddy Cow* he gives a different Glen, again a familiar motif where the rigidity of accepted codes of behaviour and the resulting lack of openness and spontaneity combine to expel the individual who cannot endure such strictness:

He got fed-up...

of tribal boundaries, of ancient household ditches
of pissing his frustration at race and religion
that walled him in.
He got fed up of being fettered in the Glen
and, bucking like a braddy cow one spring morning,
he cleared the walls and hightailed over yonder.

Perhaps there is no placename which contains more layers and nuances of meaning for Ó Searcaigh than *Bealtaine*. This is a large townland

35

between *Mín 'a Leá* and *Gort a' Choirce*. It is usually anglicised Baltoney. In local tradition it has associations with the otherworld of the Sí, a name which becomes somewhat trivialised in its usual translated form: fairies. These associations are paralleled in Gaelic tradition generally. Bealtaine was one of the main festivals in the Celtic year, May Day, the end of winter and darkness. It heralds the triumph of light and life and the arrival of growth and fertility. Not surprisingly the inhabitants of the Otherworld were extremely active on this day. Within living memory women would take their butter-making utensils to a stream where three estates had common boundary. By washing them in *Uisce na dTrí dTiarna*, the water of the three landlords, they believed their butter-making was guaranteed success for another year. This is but one illustration of many such beliefs which until recently were widely practised by the people of the Glen. Pre-Christian rituals then are part of people's lives. The month of May is linked to the cult of Mary and little altars adorned with flowers are kept in her honour during this month. Some recite the rosary at the shrines dedicated to her which are located here and there throughout the area. An awareness of these traditions increases the resonances in Ó Searcaigh's poetry since again he appropriates them to his unique voice:

In memory's album they are stored,
the curly head, the gentle eyes
and a fine May evening
but, times, I will open the mind's secrets
and I will air them in my poems,
your curly head, your gentle eyes
and a fine May evening.

Soinéad / Sonnet

The festival of Samhain must also be mentioned in this regard, the end of summer and the beginning of the rule of darkness. The dead may visit their old earthly abodes at this time and storytelling and night-visiting, the proper activities of winter, commence:

No sun visits us here
nor calls through the skylight
any season of the year.

And here in the withered world
of this foul light, it is November
for plants and lovers.

Aon Séasúr den Bhliain / Any Season of the Year.

It would be wrong however to label Cathal Ó Searcaigh a contemporary Darby O' Gill as a result of his involvement with Gaelic tradition. This is his firm base from which he explores the possibilities of many systems of belief and of ordering the universe. His place is not an obstacle but a springboard. In *Is Glas na Cnoic/Faraway Hills*, the poet confronts his sense of loneliness and estrangement in the city and succeeds in making sense of it, by feeling at home while abroad. This is an important moment in the development of any artist, where a sense of constraint is exchanged for a sense of freedom. He no longer craves the hills of home since the skyscrapers of London have taken on their dimensions.

Like a flock of sheep being driven to the mountain
The traffic is bleating
Uneasily on the roads
From Park Lane to Picadilly
And in all directions
The offices... grey green city mountains
Sun themselves and rejoice in the May sunshine,
For the first time I feel at home abroad.

He is now at home within himself regardless of his physical location. Although his terms of reference remain rooted in his rural, mountain, traditional background they now enable him to make new connections. These are nowhere more evident than in the poem *Do Jack Kerouac*. Kerouac in *On The Road* describes his journeys across America. Ó Searcaigh joins him on this odyssey again in terms of his own place:

1973. I was hooked on you. Daily I got a shot of euphoria from your work that dazzled my mind, that set my imagination soaring.

Then it was no longer Mín 'a Leá and Fána Bhuí that lay before me but the plains of Nebraska and the grasslands of Iowa.

And when I caught the blues it wasn't the Bealtaine road that stretched out in front of me but an endless American highway.

"Hey man you gotta stay high," I would stay to my friend as we freaked through the California of Cill Ulta into the Frisco of Falcarragh.

America has always been the single most important destination of Irish emigrants. It occupies a dominant place in the aspirations of those who dream of material success, as is evidenced by recent campaigns of Irish politicians to have visa allocations for their constituents increased. This symbolism has been augmented by the images of America in the cinema. The "Land of the Free" acquires new significance in the context of the poem. The freedom gained is not a release from material worry but a spiritual, artistic transcendence of the mundane. Ó Searcaigh finds America not by going to America but by recreating a land of freedom and opportunity on his own doorstep. The influence of Kerouac and the Beat poets has been very strong on Ó Searcaigh but here, he shows that he has assimilated them. He can now take them on his terms, on his turf. America is no longer the only place to be free and happy. Despite all the craven images drawing him away from his remote, backward, boggy mountain home he has realised that for him it is the source:

Here I feel the worth of poetry.
I feel my raison d'etre and importance as a person
as I became the pulse of my people's heart
and from this certainty comes peace of my mind.
My desires are tamed, my thoughts mellow
contradictions are cancelled on the spot.

In a recent anthology of Irish poetry Declan Kiberd remarks of Cathal's contemporaries: "Poets like Davitt, Rosenstock and Ní Dhomhnaill spoke for, as well as to, a wide audience, most of whose members were urban, middle-class and radical, unlike the previous generation of authors who tended to hail from the Gaeltacht or semi-Gaeltacht and to be rural, impoverished, and conservative in ideology."

Cathal Ó Searcaigh certainly fits the description for the previous generation in all but the last assertion. He is at one with his contemporaries in their concerns. Kiberd comments: "The notion that the distinction between poetry and prose is a typographical conceit is part of a much wider post-modern attempt to annul all polarities. The poets in this volume, or at least the younger among them, ask us to unlearn the illusionary differences between men and women, reason and emotion, Irish and English." Another polarity might be added to this list, that of Gaeltacht and Galltacht. For Ó Searcaigh the Gaeltacht is no gilded cage from which he can peer out at the big bad world. Like Patrick Kavanagh he had to discover the place he loved again:

They laughed at one I loved —
The triangular hill that hung
Under the Big Forth. They said
That I was bounded by the whitehorn hedges
Of the little farm and did not know the world.
But I knew that love's doorway to life
Is the same doorway everywhere.

Ashamed of what I loved
I flung her from me and called her a ditch
Although she was smiling at me with violets.

But now I am back in her briary arms
The dew of an Indian Summer morning lies
On bleached potato-stalks —
What age am I?

I do not know what age I am,
I am no mortal age;
I know nothing of women,
Nothing of cities,
I cannot die
Unless I walk outside these whitehorn hedges.

Cathal Ó Searcaigh is also strengthened and protected by his version of Kavanagh's whitehorn hedges, while the range of his poetry shows that they in no way limit him:

I see them again, love, the resplendence
I'd forgotten in the misery of the city.
Oh! don't let me stray again:
Shelter me here between the bright causeway of your legs,
Add a fresh dimension to my poem.

Cor Úr / A Fresh Dimension

The word destiny may be substituted for poem in the last line. This dimension is already manifested in recent work of Cathal, some of which is published in this volume for the first time. Della Terza supplies us with another insight: "Rocco's poetry is the centre where the problems of his existence converge, the place where the different patterns of his behaviour can be discerned and analysed." Cathal Ó Searcaigh brings us into that centre in these poems. They are the fruit of the seeds planted many years ago and we are invited to partake. I hope you will be enriched and rewarded by your response.

Lillis Ó Laoire   *Lá Bealtaine, 1992*

40

Do Mháire Mhac an tSaoi

"Cuirfidh sé brí ionat agus beatha,"
arsa sean-Bhríd, faghairt ina súile
ag tabhairt babhla fíoruisce chugam
as an tobar is glaine i nGleann an Átha.
Tobar a coinníodh go slachtmhar
ó ghlúin go glúin, oidhreacht
luachmhar an teaghlaigh
cuachta istigh i gclúid foscaidh,
claí cosanta ina thimpeall
leac chumhdaigh ar a bhéal.

Agus mé ag teacht i méadaíocht
anseo i dtús na seascaidí
ní raibh teach sa chomharsanacht
gan a mhacasamhail de thobar,
óir cúis mhaíte ag achan duine
an t-am adaí a fholláine is a fhionnuaire
a choinníodh sé tobar a mhuintire:
ní ligfí sceo air ná smál
is dá mbeadh rian na ruamheirge
le feiceáil ann, le buicéad stáin
dhéanfaí é a thaoscadh ar an bhall
is gach ráithe lena choinneáil folláin
chumhraítí é le haol áithe.

Uisce beo bíogúil, fíoruisce glé
a d'fhoinsigh i dtobar ár dteaghlaigh.
I gcannaí agus i gcrúiscíní
thóg siad é lá i ndiaidh lae
agus nuair a bhíodh íota tarta orthu
i mbrothall an tsamhraidh

THE WELL

For Máire Mhac an tSaoi

" ' Twill put a stir in you, and life,'
says old Bridget, spark in her eyes
proffering a bowl of spring-water
from the purest well in Gleann an Átha,
a well that was tended tastily
from generation to generation, the precious
heritage of the household
snugly sheltered in a nook,
a ditch around it for protection,
a flagstone on its mouth.

When I was growing up
here in the early 'sixties
there wasn't a house in the neighbourhood
without its like,
for everyone was proud then
of how wholesome and pure
they kept the family well:
they wouldn't let it become murky or slimy
and at the first traces of red-rust
it was bailed-out with a tin bucket
then purified every season with kiln-lime.

Lively, living water, pellucid spring-water
gushed forth from our family well.
In tin-cans and pitchers
they drew it daily
and in the devouring thirst
of sweltering summer
it slaked and cooled them
in field and bog.
It was a tonic, too,

thugadh fliuchadh agus fuarú daofa
i bpáirceanna agus i bportaigh.
Deoch íce a bhí ann fosta
a chuir ag preabadaigh iad le haoibhneas
agus mar uisce ionnalta
d'fhreastail ar a gcás ó bhreith go bás.

Ach le fada tá uisce reatha
ag fiaradh chugainn isteach
ó chnoic i bhfad uainn
is i ngach cisteanach
ar dhá thaobh an ghleanna
scairdeann uisce as sconna
uisce lom gan loinnir
a bhfuil blas searbh súlaigh air
is i measc mo dhaoine
tá tobar an fhíoruisce ag dul i ndíchuimhne.

"Is doiligh tobar a aimsiú faoi láthair,"
arsa Bríd, ag líonadh an bhabhla athuair.
"Tá siad folaithe i bhfeagacha agus i bhféar,
tachtaithe ag caileannógach agus cuiscreach,
ach in ainneoin na neamhairde go léir
níor chaill siad a dhath den tseanmhianach.
Aimsigh do thobar féin, a chroí,
óir tá am an anáis romhainn amach:
Caithfear pilleadh arís ar na foinsí."

that made them throb with delight
and for their ablutions
it served from cradle to grave.

But, this long time, piped water from distant hills
sneaks into every kitchen
on both sides of the glen;
water spurts from a tap,
mawkish, without sparkle,
zestless as slops
and among my people
the springwell is being forgotten.

" 'Tis hard to find a well nowadays",
says Bridget filling the bowl again.
"They're hidden in rushes and grass,
choked by green scum and ferns,
but, despite the neglect,
they've lost none of their true mettle.
Seek out your own well, my dear,
for the age of want is near:
There will have to be a going back to sources."

translated by Gabriel Fitzmaurice.

Do Heather Allen

Istigh anseo in ísleán an tsléibhe
tá sé níos suaimhní ná séipéal tuaithe.
Siúlaim, bearád i bpóca, go tostach
síos cairpéad caonaigh na pasáide,
síos idir na piúnna tortógacha,
is ag ardán na haltóra, seasaim bomaite,
is beochán beag gaoithe — an cléireach —
ag croitheadh túise fraoigh ar fud na háite.

Ach i séipéal seo an tsléibhe níl trácht
ar riail ná ar reacht is ní bhím cráite
ag cráifeacht bhorb na puilpide
ag bagairt léin ar lucht na hearráide.
Ní Dia na nDeor ná Dia na nDealg
Dia na Tíorántachta ná Dia na Trócaire
an Dia seo ar a bhfuil mé anois ag faire
ach Dia gur cuma leis mo chabhair nó mo chealg.

Anseo is lena bheatha seachas lena bhriathra
a chuireann cibé Dia atá ann é féin in iúl;
gan aird aige ar chomharthaí ómóis ach oiread le haltú.
Foinse gach fuinnimh. Cruthaitheoir na nDúl.
Is leor leis a bheith ag borradh, ag bláthú
is ag brú chun solais i ngach brobh nuafháis.
Tá sé ag aoibhniú chugam i niamh gach datha
ag beoú an aeir faram lena bheatha.

Le gach anáil dá dtarraingím,
análaím chugam é ar an aer íon
chomh friseáilte le harán, chomh fionnuar le fíon.

SANCTUARY

For Heather Allen

Here in the hollow of the mountains
it is more peaceful than a country chapel.
I walk, cap in pocket, silently
down the mossy carpet of the aisle,
down between the grass-clump pews,
and at the altar-height, stand a moment,
while a faint breeze — the altar-boy —
dispenses heather incense everywhere.

Yet in this mountain chapel there's no talk
of rule or regulation and I'm not plagued
by the brutal piety of the pulpit
threatening those who err with torment.
This is no God of Tears or God of Thorns,
God of Tyranny or God of Mercy
this God I am now looking at
but a God indifferent to my hindrance or my help.

Here it is with his life rather than his words
that whatever God there is makes himself known;
ignoring signs of reverence, veneration.
The source of all energy. Creator of the Elements.
Enough for him to stir, blossom
and push towards the light in every new-grown shoot.
His joy is the lustre of every colour,
he gives life to the air around me with his life.

With every breath I take
I breathe him from the pure air
as fresh as new-baked bread, as cool as wine.

translated by Aodán Mac Póilín

47

Do Lillis Ó Laoire

Is cuimhneach liom Domhnach fadó fadó. Domhnach síoraí samhraidh a bhí ann. Chuaigh mé ar thuras i ngluaisteán gorm. Turas chun an tSolais.

Cealaíodh am agus aimsear; clog agus caileandar. Bhí mé ag tiomáint sa tsíoraíocht. Dia a bhí ionam ar deoraíocht.

Bhí sé te. I bhfíor-dhuibheagán na bhflaitheas thum mé "sponge" mo shamhlaíochta is nuair a d'fhaisc mé é ina dhiaidh sin filíocht a tháinig ag sileadh as. Filíocht a thug fliuchadh agus fuaradh.

Bhí an féar ag ceiliúr is ag ceol ar na crainn. Bhí na héanacha ag éirí glas sna cuibhrinn. Bhí na néalta ag méileach ar na bánta. Ní raibh oiread agus caora le feiceáil sa spéir.

Casadh sruthán orm a bhí ag fáil bháis leis an tart. Thosaigh mé ag caoineadh is tháinig sé chuige féin go tapaidh. Thóg mé cnoc beag a bhí ag siúl ar thaobh an bhealaigh. Dúirt sé go raibh sé ag déanamh cúrsa i dtarrtháil sléibhe. Is cuimhneach liom gur fhág sé a chaipín ceo ina dhiaidh sa charr.

Ach dúirt an ghaoth liom a casadh orm i mbarr an Ghleanna go raibh sí ag gabháil an treo sin níos déanaí is go dtabharfadh sí an caipín ceo arís chuige. An ghaoth bhocht. Tháinig mé uirthi go tobann. Bhí sí nocht. Ach chomh luath agus a chonaic sí mé tharraing sí an t-aer thart uirthi féin go cúthalach agus labhair sí liom go séimh.

Bhí siad uilig chomh cineálta céanna. Thug na clocha cuireadh domh suí ina gcuideachta is nuair a chiúnaigh siad thart orm go cainteach thuig mé cad is tost ann. D'éist mé le bláth beag bhí ag seinm "sonata" ar "phiano" a piotail, ceol a chuir aoibhneas ar mo shrón. Tharraing an loch mo phictúir.

ON SUCH A DAY

For Lillis Ó Laoire.

I remember one Sunday long ago. An eternal Summer Sunday. I went on a journey in a blue car. A journey towards the Light.

Time and weather were no more; clock and calendar. I was driving in eternity. I was God wandering.

It was hot. In the depths of heaven I plunged the sponge of my imagination and when I squeezed it afterwards poetry flowed from it. Poetry that wet and cooled me.

The grass was warbling and singing on the trees. The birds were greening in the fields. The clouds were bleating in the pastures. Not one sheep was in the sky.

I chanced upon a stream that was dying of thirst. I began to cry and it recovered quickly. I picked up a small hill that was walking by the wayside. It said it was doing a course in mountain-rescue. I remember it left its cap behind in the car.

But the wind I met at the top of the Glen said she was going that way later and would return the cap to him. The poor wind! I came upon her suddenly. She was sunning herself at the top of the Glen. She was naked. But the instant she saw me, she drew the air shyly around her and spoke gently.

They were all as kind as she. The stones invited me into their company and when they quietened talkatively about me I understood the meaning of silence. I listened to a small flower playing a sonata on her petal-piano, music that pleased my nose. The lake drew my picture.

Agus an lá, fear tí an tSolais, cuimhneoidh mé air go brách. Bhí sé chomh béasach dea-mhúinte agus é i mbun gnó; ag freastal is ag friotháladh ar mo chuid riachtanaisí. Níor dhruid sé na doirse is níor tharraing sé na dallóga go dtí gur dhúirt mé leis go raibh mé ag gabháil 'na bhaile. D'oibrigh sé uaireanta breise go díreach ar mhaithe liomsa.

Agus tháinig an oíche 'na bhaile i mo chuideachta, a corp slim sleamhain ag sioscadh i mo thimpeall; spéarthaí dubha a gúna ag caitheamh drithlí chugam. Mheall sí mé lena glórthaí.

Is cuimhneach liom Domhnach fadó fadó is cé go bhfuil luanscrios déanta air ó shoin

Creidim i gcónaí sna míorúiltí.

And the day, host of the Light, I'll remember forever. He was so well-mannered and polite doing his duty; attending to and anticipating my needs. He didn't close the doors nor pull the blinds till I informed him I was going home. He worked overtime just for my benefit.

And night came home with me, her sleek and slender body rustling about me; the black skies of her dress twinkling all around me. She enthralled me with the sound of her voice.

I remember that Sunday long long ago. And though time has destroyed it.

I believe in miracles still.

translated by Gabriel Fitzmaurice.

do Anraí Mac Giolla Chomhaill

"Sin clábar! Clábar cáidheach,
a chuilcigh," a dúirt m'athair go bagrach
agus mé ag slupairt go súgach
i ndíobhóg os cionn an bhóthair.
"Amach leat as do chuid clábair
sula ndéanfar tú a chonáil!"

Ach choinnigh mé ag spágáil agus ag splaiseáil
agus ag scairtigh le lúcháir:
"Clábar! Clábar! Seo mo chuid clábair!"
Cé nár chiallaigh an focal faic i mo mheabhair
go dtí gur mhothaigh mé i mo bhuataisí glugar
agus trí gach uile líbín de mo cheirteacha
creathanna fuachta na tuisceana.

A chlábar na cinniúna, bháigh tú mo chnámha.

WHEN I WAS THREE

For Anraí Mac Giolla Chomhaill

"That's muck! Filthy muck, you little scamp,'
my father was so severe in speech
while I was messing happily
in my mud-trench by the road.
'Out with you from that muck
before you freeze to death!'

But I continued shuffling, having fun,
all the time screaming with delight:
"Muck! Muck! It's my own muck!"
But the word was nothing in my innocence
until I felt the squelch of wellies
and, through the dripping wet of clothes,
the shivering knowledge of water.

Ah! Muck of destiny, you drenched my bones!

translated by Thomas Mc Carthy

Do Murray Learmont

Is cuimhneach liom an fathach sneachta
a ghealaigh chugainn ó Ardán Aindí
maidin gheimhridh i naoi déag seasca a trí
agus mé féin is na Gallchóraigh
ag déanamh cuideachta sa tsneachta.

Is cuimhneach liom an chuil cholgach
a bhí ar bhuidéal bhriste a bhéil agus é
ár ngrinniú leis an tsúil chré
a dhubhaigh as ceartlár a éadain
díreach os cionn chuthrán a ghaosáin.

Is cuimhneach liom an lá is an rírá
a bhí againne ag bocléimnigh is ag scairtigh
thart air go háthasach; adhraitheoirí
ag móradh is ag moladh na híomhá
a thaibhsigh as diamhracht na hoíche.

Is cuimhneach liom an scáth arrachtach
a chaith sé tharainn le héirí gealaí,
ár dtarraingt chuige isteach is mar d'éalaigh
muid abhaile, creathnaithe roimh an neach
a bhí ag iarraidh muid a fhuadach.

Is cuimhneach liom an scread choscrach
a tháinig asainn nuair nach raibh sé romhainn
an mhaidin ghéar ghréine dár gcionn
is mar chuartaigh muid go mion
is go cruinn na coiscéimeanna bána a shleamhnaigh uainn.

For Murray Learmont

I remember the snow-giant
that shimmered for us from Ardán Aindí
one winter morning in nineteen-sixty-three
while the Gallaghers and I
were amusing ourselves in the snow.

I remember the angry look
on the broken bottle of his mouth
while he scrutinized us with an earthy eye
that blackened from the dead-centre of his forehead
right above the turf-sod of his nose.

I remember the day and the hubbub
we had bucklepping and shrieking
around him with joy, worshippers
extolling and praising the image
that appeared from the mysterious night.

I remember the monstrous shadow
he cast over us at the rising of the moon
luring us to him, and how we fled
home, trembling before the being
who would abduct us.

I remember our screech of distress
when he had disappeared
the following sun-sharp morning
and how we searched high and low
for white footsteps that eluded us.

Ó is cuimhneach liom ár gcaill go fóill
ag amharc oraibhse a ógánacha an cheoil
ag coinneáil cuideachta ansiúd thall
le bhur n-arrachta sneachta, bhur bhfeart aon lae
a imeos le teacht na gréine ar ball

gan oiread is lorg coise a fhágáil ina dhiaidh.

Oh! I remember the day of our loss yet,
watching you, singing children
amusing yourselves yonder
with your abominable snowman, creation-of-a-day
that will disappear at sunrise

leaving no footprint behind.

translated by Gabriel Fitzmaurice

SNEACHTA

Do Tom Walsh

D'éalaínn amach le teacht an lae
ar na maidneacha geala geimhridh adaí
is an sneachta ag titim mar chlúmh gé.

Bhíodh an tír chomh coimhthíoch le fásach;
na harda uilig ina ndumhcha is na bóithigh
cuachta go cruiteach, camaill chodlatacha.

Ba mhór an tógáil croí ar maidin go luath
an bhalbh-bháine adaí a bheith i mo thimpeall
is an saol á shamhlú agam ansiúd as an nua.

Tá an leathanach bán seo dálta thír an tsneachta
ag mealladh an pháiste atá istigh amach
lena chuma féin a chur ar lom na cruthaitheachta.

For Tom Walsh

I used slip out at daybreak
those bright winter mornings;
snow falling like goose-down.

The land strange as a desert;
the hills all sand-dunes, and the byres
humped, huddled, sleepy camels.

Those early mornings filled me with exhilaration —
dumb whiteness all around
and the world imagined anew.

This white page, like the snow-land
tempts the child within
to put his own stamp on blank creation.

translated by Aodán Mac Póilín

DATHANNA

(Dán do pháistí)

Teastaíonn ó mo chuid dathanna deá-mhéin
agus teangmháil a chothú lena macasamhail féin —

I gcanúint ghlas shochmaidh
freagraíonn an féar
glas smaragóide mo gheansaí.

Tá donn ciabhach mo ghruaige
ag cur bhur dtuairisce
a dhlaíoga fraoigh na Mucaise.

Ó bhláthanna an chrainn úll
titeann beannachtaí go binn
ar bhándearg mo chraicinn.

Tá an sceach gheal ag cogarnaí
le gile mo bhrístí. Tá aoibh aoldaite
ar an chlaí atá i m'aice.

Ar théada tinnealacha an cheatha
tig sreangscéalta seirce
chuig mo shúile ó ghorm na spéire.

Tá daol dubh ag déanamh spraoi
le duibhe mo bhuaitisí. Scairteann
cnapán súiche leo ó chúl an tí —

Anois tá an t-aer ar bharr amháin creatha,
Mothaím tarraingteacha aisteacha i mo bheatha:

Á! I ngach ceann de na ceithre hairde
tá mo chuid dathanna ag déanamh cairde.

(A poem for children)

My colours wish to mate
With kindred spirits and communicate —

In the soft green dialect
the grass answers
to my emerald gansey.

My flaring brown hair
is asking for you:
heather-tresses of Mucais.

From apple-tree blossoms
blessings sweetly fall
on my skin's pinkness.

The hawthorn whispers
to my pants' brightness;
limewashed smile of nearby wall.

On tense wires of rain
telegrams carry love
to my eyes out of the blue.

A beetle plays with the blackness
of my boots. A lump of soot
gives a shout behind the house.

Now the air is all a-tremble,
My life is filled with strange attractions:

Ah! From here to where the world ends
All my colours are making friends.

translated by Gabriel Rosenstock

Do Mhicheál Ó Domhnaill

Ag síobshiúl ó mhaidin ar an bhóthar go Londain
mothaím sú an tsamhraidh ag cuisliú i ngach ní.
Á! Féach! Faoi spreagadh steall gréine tá burdúin
á gceapadh ag cnaipí práis mo bhrístí.

Ar bhruach an bhealaigh mhóir is an tráthnóna
ina phléaráca ó rírá na tráchta;
i mo shuí ar mo phaca, m'órdóg ag preabadh go beoga
mar loinneog in amhrán mó shiúlta.

Is mo chaorshnó déagóra chomh glé le fógra
ach má thiomáineann siad tharam ní bhímse míshásta
óir i mo fhoighdese tá fairsinge Sahára.

Is nach aoibhinn mar chóiríonn giollaí gréine in ór mé.
Ó, táimse i m'ór-uige chomh mórluachach le Rí, cé
go bhfuilimse ar tí bheith i dtuilleamaí na déirce.

MA BOHÉME

For Micheál Ó Domhnaill

As I hitch the road to London in the morning
I feel the summer juices throbbing in all things.
Ah, look! A shaft of sun arouses the brass buttons
Of my jeans to make free verse.

On the side of the highway as the evening
Rowdies to the heavy-metal of the traffic;
I sit on my pack, my thumb erect
And swinging like the chorus of a marching song.

My berry-red youthful face gives a clear mesage
But if they drive on past I'm not unhappy
Since my patience is as wide as the Sahara.

Oh, the bliss as the sun arrays me in gold —
In my cloth-of-gold I have a princely style
Although I come close to having to look for hand-outs.

translated by Gréagóir Ó Dúill

63

Blaisim ar uairibh
i maistreadh sráide
babhla bláiche
i riocht dáin.

HIGH STREET, KENSINGTON, 6 P.M.

There are times I taste
in the street's churning
a bowl of buttermilk
in the shape of a poem.

translated by Gabriel Fitzmaurice

MAIGDILÉANA

Do Michael agus Ann Ferry

I dtrátha an ama a dtachtann sealán aibhléise
aoibh shoilseach na spéire
tím uaim í de ghnáth, an ghirseach is deise
de mhná sráide na háite seo;
agus í ar a *beat* ag *cruiseáil* go huaigneach
sa mharbhsholas chnámhach
ag spléachadh go fáilí ar scáilí na gcros teilifíse
ag cuartú a Calvaire go heaglach.

Amantaí eile tím í le haithne an lae
agus í i gcaifitéire ag ól tae
sula bpilleann sí ar an *underground*
abhaile ina haonar go Paddington.
Nuair nach labhraíonn éinne leat, a ghrá,
thíos ansiúd, dubh bán nó riabhach
bhéarfaidh na fógraí béal bán duit agus béadán
i dtumba folamh an *underground*

nó b'fhéidir scéala ón Ghalailéach.

MAGDALENE

ForMichael and Ann Ferry

About the time the noose of electric light chokes
the luminous beauty of the sky,
I see her usually, the loveliest young girl
of the ladies-of-the-night around here,
on her beat cruising lonely
in the skeletal half-light,
glimpsing on walls the crosses of T.V. aerials
as she seeks her Calvary in fear.

At other times I see her at break of day
in a cafe drinking tea
before she returns on the Underground
home alone to Paddington.
When nobody speaks to you, love,
down there, black, white or in-between,
the ads will softsoap you with gossip
in the empty tomb of the Underground

or maybe bear tidings of the Galilean.

translated by Gabriel Fitzmaurice

Do Angela Carter

Tá mé ag fanacht ar dhuine inteacht
le teacht na hoíche.
Anseo i gceartlár Phiccadilly, thart
fá bhéal bagrach an fhostaisiún
tá fuacht feanntach na gaoithe
ag cur greadfach ionam faoi sheacht.
Tá ochlán an ocrais i mo phutóga
is na néaróga luaile as tiúin
agus tusa
tusa a bhfuil do bhéal lán de phóga,
cá bhfuil tú agus an uair ann?
Dá rachainn ag cuartú cuidithe,
Dá dtitfinn ar mo dhá ghlúin
anseo díreach in áit na mbonn
an dtiocfadh coimhthíoch an chroí mhóir
chugam de choiscéim chiúin
ó na daoine dúrúnta seo
na daoine deifreacha déanfasacha seo
a chuireann cor bealaigh orthu féin
le mé a sheachaint go giorraisc
amhail is dá mba poll bréan
a bhí rompu ar an chosán?
Is smaointím anois
ar Joe Beag i bProchlais
a chomhairligh domh lá amháin
sular fhág mé m'áit dhúchais:
"Más lámh chuidithe atá uait, a stócaigh
gheobhaidh tú an ceann is úsáidtí
sáite ar cheann do sciatháin."
Ó Dia go deo le tarrtháil na híoróine.

68

For Angela Carter

I am waiting for somebody
in the dusk.
Here in the centre of Piccadilly, around
the menacing mouth of the Underground
a cold nippy wind
bites into me savagely;
hunger gnaws at my guts,
my limbs are gone jittery
and you
you with your mouthful of kisses
where are you, now the hour having struck?
If I looked for kindliness,
If I collapsed in a heap
here, right here where I'm standing
would some big-hearted stranger
step forward benignly
from these sullen Londoners,
these hurrying, self-conceited Londoners
who slip by me, curtly
as if I were a cess-pit
befouling their way?
And I recall immediately
Joe Beag in Prochlais
giving his timely advice before
I left my home and my country:
"If you ever need a helping hand, lad
you will always find the most reliable one
secured to the end of your arm".
Thank God for the saving grace of irony.

Ach gurb é a leithéidí
cé a dhéanfadh mé a ghiúmaráil
ar uair seo na himní.
Tá mé ag fanacht ar dhuine inteacht
le teacht na hoíche,
ag éisteacht le rac 'n' rol na gcaogadaí
Buddy Holly agus Chuck Berry
ag *tump*áil ó bhoth bídh ar an tsráid.
Tá aoibh ainglí as Botticelli
anois ag gabháil thar bráid
is tá fáinleoga ar eiteog
i bflip-fleaip a cuid bróg,
ach mar an t-aon hairt i bpáca cártaí
suaitear í as amharc
i gcleas láimhe de chuid na cinniúna.
Tá cruiteachán ag buscáil
ar thaobh an fhoscaidh den choirnéal
i Regent Street Íochtarach;
a shacsafón snagach
mar pheata madaidh ag caoineadh
i m*bedsit* a tréigeadh.
Ós ár gcionn, tá
flaitheas teicnidhaite na fógraíochta
is seacht dtíolacaí an eolais
ag teacht anuas ina dteangacha solais
ó Spiorad Naomh na Siopadóireachta.
"You wanta make it, dontcha?"
arsa leadhb i ngúna gairid;
cling-cleaing scipéad airgid
ina canúint bhréag-Mheiriceánach.
I ré seo na mBréag
téann na striapacha tharam go sotalach

70

Without its blessings
where would I get an uplift
in this hour of anxiety.
I am waiting for somebody
in the dusk,
listening to fifties rock 'n' roll
Buddy Holly and Chuck Berry
thumping from a street vendor's foodstall.
An angelic face out of a Botticelli
now passes by;
there are swallows in flight
in the flip-flap of her shoes
but like the ace of hearts in a pack of cards
she is shuffled out of sight
by fate's sleight of hand trick.
A hunchback busker
plays on the sheltery side of the corner
in Lower Regent Street;
the jazz sobs of his saxophone
like a pet dog whimpering
in a deserted bedsit.
Above us
the technicolor heaven of advertising
and the seven gifts of knowledge
pour down in tongues of light
from the Holy Spirit of Consumerism.
"You wanta make it dontcha"
says a skimpily clad tart,
the cling-clang of a cash register
in her pseudo-American drawl.
In this age of deceit
the whores parade by, cocksure,

mar chathuithe Chríost san fhásach:
á ngrá leo ar bharra a ngéag;
is mothaím fuacht ar fud m'inchinne
díobháil nach bhfuil aon duine siosmaideach
le spréach a chur i m'intleacht;
Is meabhraím go hamaideach
arbh fhearr athrú aeráide,
sloig de Phuins na Fírinne
nó Aspro beag Inspioráide
le mo chothromaíocht a chur i gceart.
Tá mé ag fanacht ar dhuine inteacht
le teacht na hoíche,
ag éisteacht i mo shamhlaíocht
le glaoch na gcnoc is na gcaorán
ó Mhín 'a Leá is ó Mhín na Craoibhe
Ó Phrochlais is ón Dúnán.
Níl de chara ag Cumhaidh ach Cuimhne
ach mar ghrianghraf a fhliuchfaí
tá sin féin ag gabháil as aithne
i dtruacántas.
Ó a Dhia na nGrás
an bhfuil aon dul as
seachas lámh a chur i mo bhás
mar a rinne Celan agus Berryman
ach i mo chroí istigh
tá fhios agam go rí-mhaith
nach doras éalaithe ar bith an féin-bhás
ach íomhá
de dhoras péinteáilte ar bhallaí na Díomá
ach ina dhiaidh sin agus uile
is doiligh an duairceas seo a chloí,

72

like Christ's temptations in the desert,
their hearts on their sleeves;
And my mind chills
for no kind friend comes
to kindle the damp tinder of my intellect
and I reflect a little frivolously
which would be better, a change of climate,
a swig of the punch of Truth
or a wee Aspro of inspiration
to straighten out my disorders.
I am waiting for somebody
in the dusk,
yearning in my imagination
for the call of the hills and the bogs
from Mín 'a Leá and from Mín na Craoibhe
from Prochlais and from Dúnán.
I am alone and alone has no friend
but memory, but memory is a snap-shot
that wept upon, goes out of focus,
blurs.
Oh Good God
is there any escape route
other than the suicidal one
taken by Celan and Berryman
but deep in my heart
I know full well
that suicide is no escape door
only the image
of a door painted on the walls of Despair.
But despite all that
it's difficult to overcome this ominous gloom

mise
a bhí comh aerach anuraidh
le ceo an Earraigh
ag déanamh Caidhp an Chúil Aird
ar bharr an Eargail
ach anois is cosúla
seideog de bhonnán árthaigh
leis an chneadán seo i mo scornaí
is mé ag cur garr mo chroí amach
sáraithe
i dtoitcheo na cathrach.
Tá mé ag fanacht ar dhuine inteacht
le teacht na hoíche.
Ó a Dhia na bhFeart
tuigim anois agus choíche
cumhaidh agus crá croí an aonaráin
is mé imithe chun seachráin
ar an fhóidín mearaí seo i bPiccadilly
i measc daoine atá ar dhíth a ndúchais;
is ní aon ábhar iontais
a bheith ag meabhrú idir mionnaí móra
go mbeidh an chathair seo domhsa i gconaí
amhail Gort an Chriadóra
a ceannaíodh le airgead Iúdais
mar áit adhlactha do choimhthígh.
Tá mé ag fanacht ar dhuine inteacht
le teacht na hoíche,
ag fanacht is ag fanacht
mar bheadh an guthán ag ringeáil
i mbosca folamh an choirnéil;
mar bheadh an damhán alla

74

in myself, I
who a year ago was as lively
as the spring mist
dancing the High Caul Cap
on the top of Errigal.
But now
the groan of a ship's siren
is closer to this gasping in my throat
and no matter how hard I try
I'm left floundering
in the exhaust fumes of the city.
I'm waiting for somebody
in the dusk.
Almighty God
I understand finally
the homesickness and heartbreak of the exile
having myself gone astray
on this mind-disordering spot in Piccadilly
amongst people deprived of their patrimony
and here I am
thinking amidst my profanities
that this city will always be for me
like the potter's field
bought with Judas' blood money
as a graveyard for the abandoned.
I am waiting for somebody
in the dusk
waiting and waiting
like that phone ringing
in the empty booth of the corner;
like the spider

cuachta i ngreasán ar an bhalla;
mar bheadh an madadh duiseachta
ansiúd ag síneadh a mhuineáil;

mar an file lena chuid focla.

crouched there in his web on the wall;
like that pointer dog
craning his neck;

like the poet with his words.

translated by Gréagóir Ó Dúill

Do Bhrian, Bríd agus Caitlín

Am stad. Amach leis an iomlán againn sciob sceab.
Pláigh chuileog as carn lofa d'oifigí gnó.
Níl éinne fial le dáimh ach í siúd thall — Báb
i mbreacsholas an chlóis chaoich. *"I'm Nano*
the Nympho," arsa mana griogach a cíoch.
"Bí ar d'fhaichill uirthi," a dúradh go fuarchúiseach.
"Tá fabht inti," is brúim isteach i gceann de thithe
gabh-i-leith-chugam na bPizzas mar rogha ar an striapach.

Níl le feiceáil anseo ach feidhmeannaigh oifige.
Scaoth ag gach bord. Seabhrán os cionn na mbiachlár.
Samhnasach. Urlacaim, sconnóg ar mhuin sconnóige
lá domlasach na hoifige. Gach uile eiseamláir
mhífholláin a ndearnas díleá air le bheith i mo *bhoss;*
gach scig-gháire pislíneach faoi mé bheith *très*
distingué i mo chulaith úr cheant; gach seal ar an *doss*
le héalú ó cheirnín scríobhtha a bhféinspéise — mé — mé — mé.

Damnú orthu. ní dhéanfadsa bábántacht níos mó
ar theoiricí míofara as broinn tí chuntais. Go hifreann
le gach *clic — cleaic — ac* as clóscríobhán Miss Devereaux;
le gach *jolly good delineation, pop it up to Dodo or Boremann;*
le gach luas staighre, le gach clagairt chloig, le gach *ditto;*
leo siúd go léir a d'angaigh mo mhéinse le bliain. Amárach
pillfidh mé ar Ghleann an Átha, áit a nglanfar sileadh an anró
as m'aigne, áit a gcuirfear in iúl domh go carthanach

go gcneasaíonn goin ach nach bhfásann fionnadh ar an cholm.

For Brian, Bríd and Caitlín

Knocking-off time. We all swarm out.
A plague of flies from a dunghill of offices.
No giving or warmth, but from that one — the Dolly-bird
in the half-light of a dead-end. "I'm Nano
the Nympho" emblazoned over her breasts.
"Watch out for her," someone says casually.
"She's risky," and I turn towards
a come-hither Pizza Parlour instead of the whore.

Nothing here but office flunkies.
Seething around the tables. Buzzing over the menus.
Disgusting. I vomit, retch after retch
the bilious office day. Every unwholesome thing
I digested to be a boss;
every drivelling snigger that I'm *très*
distingué in my new jumble-sale suit; every doss
escaping the scratched record of their egotism - me - me - me.

Damn them. I'll no longer tug my forelock
to loathsome theories from the womb of a counting house. To hell
with every click — clack — ack of Miss Devereaux' typewriter;
with every "jolly good delineation, pop it up to Dodo or Boremann;"
with every moving stair, every clattering bell, every ditto;
with all that festered in my spirit for a year. Tomorrow
I'll return to Gleann an Átha where this ooze of despair will be drained
from my mind, where I'll be told, with kindness

That the wound heals but that no hair grows on the scar.

translated by Aodán Mac Póilín

Do Rachel Brown

Triallfaidh mé le mo chrá amárach ar thearmann
anonn thar fhraoch na farraige;
óir chan fhuil fáil i reilig bhrocach na n-árasán
ar a bhfuil curtha anseo de m'óige.

Ansiúd thall tá seanteallach foscailte an chineáltais
agus tinidh chroíúil na fáilte;
ansiúd tá teangaidh sholásach ina cógas leighis
le léim a chur arís i mo shláinte.

Ó triallfaidh mé ar thearmann na coimirce anonn
agus dóchas ag bolgadh i mo sheolta;
áit a bhfaighidh mé goradh agus téarnamh ann
ó fhuaraíocht thuamúil na sráide.

For Rachel Brown

To-morrow I travel on to a haven
Beyond the pitch and brawl of the sea:
The flats round here are a run-down graveyard
Where my young self walks like a nameless zombie.

In an open house over there, the hearth
Is the heart and soul of every welcome;
When I hear that candid, soothing accent
I'll be flush with health and my step will quicken.

O I'm travelling on to a sheltering haven
And hope is bellying out in my sail.
In a warmer place, I'll mend and be safe
From streets as cold as the wind round headstones.

translated by Seamus Heaney

Inár seomra suí leapa
seargann na plandaí tí
fiú i dtús an tSamhraidh.

Titeann duilleoga feoite
i measc deora taisligh
dusta agus proinn dhóite.

Ní ghlaonn an ghrian
isteach trí fhuinneog an dín
aon séasúr den bhliain.

Is anseo i saol seargtha
an bhrocsholais, tá sé ina Shamhain
ag plandaí is ag leannáin.

In our bed-sitting room
the house-plants wither
even in early summer.

Leaves shrivel and fall
amid the dampness
the dust and the burnt meals.

No sun visits us here
nor calls through the skylight
any season of the year.

And here in the withered world
of this foul light, it is November
for plants and lovers.

translated by Aodán Mac Póilín

PORTRÁID DEN GHABHA
MAR EALAÍONTÓIR ÓG

Do Mháire Nic Suibhne

Tá mé dúthuirseach de Dhún Laoghaire,
de mo sheomra suí leapa in Ascal an Chrosaire.
Áit chúng a chraplaíonn mo chuid oibre
mar ghabha focal
is a fhágann mé istoíche go dearóil
ag brú gaoil ar lucht óil
seachas a bheith ag casúireacht dánta do mo dhaoine
ar inneoin m'inchinne.
A Dhia na bhfeart, tá sé imithe thar fóir
an díomhaointeas damanta seo!
Á! Dá mbeinn arís i gCaiseal na gCorr
ní i mo chiotachán a bheinn, leathbheo.

Ní hé leoga! Ach i gceárta na teanga
bheinnse go breabhsánta
ag cleachtadh mo cheirde gach lá;
ar bhoilg m'aigne ag tathant bruíne
ag gríosú smaointe chun spréiche
ag casúracht go hard
caint mhiotalach mo dhaoine.

A PORTRAIT OF THE BLACKSMITH
AS A YOUNG ARTIST

For Máire Nic Suibhne

I'm sick and tired of Dún Laoghaire,
Of my bedsit in Cross's Avenue,
A pokey place that cripples my wordsmith's craft
And leaves me nightly in the dumps
Scrounging kindred among the drunks
Instead of hammering poems for my people
On the anvil of my mind.
Almighty God! It's gone too far,
This damned silence.
If I were back in Caiseal na gCorr
I'd not be awkward, half-alive.

No way! But in the smithy of my tongue
I'd be hale and hearty
Working at my craft daily
Inciting the bellows of my mind
Stirring thoughts to flame
Hammering loudly
The mettlesome speech of my people.

translated by Gabriel Fitzmaurice

Ciúnaíonn tú chugam as ceo na maidine
mus na raideoige ar d' fhallaing fraoigh,
do ghéaga ina srutháin gheala ag sní
thart orm go lúcháireach, géaga
a fháiltíonn romham le fuiseoga.

Féachann tú orm anois go glé
le lochanna móra maorga do shúl
Loch an Ghainimh ar deis, Loch Altáin ar clé,
gach ceann acu soiléir, lán den spéir
agus snua an tsamhraidh ar a ngruanna.

Agus scaoileann tú uait le haer an tsléibhe
crios atá déanta as ceo bruithne na Bealtaine
scaoileann tú uait é, a rún mo chléibhe,
ionas go bhfeicim anois ina n-iomláine
críocha ionúine do cholainne

ó Log Dhroim na Gréine go hAlt na hUillinne
ón Mhalaidh Rua go Mín na hUchta,
thíos agus thuas, a chorp na háilleachta
gach cuar agus cuas, gach ball gréine,
gach ball seirce a bhí imithe i ndíchuimhne

ó bhí mé go deireanach i do chuideachta.
Tím iad arís, a chroí, na niamhrachtaí
a dhearmadaigh mé i ndíbliú na cathrach.
Ó ná ceadaigh domh imeacht arís ar fán:
clutharaigh anseo mé idir chabhsaí geala do chos,
deonaigh cor úr a chur i mo dhán.

Like silence you come from the morning mist,
musk of bog-myrtle on your heather cloak,
your limbs — bright streams lapping joyfully
around me, limbs
that welcome me with skylarks.

You see me truly
in the majestic lakes of your eyes —
Loch an Ghainimh on the right, Loch Altán on the left,
both plainly visible, full of sky,
the complexion of summer on their cheeks.

And you loosen to the mountain air
your girdle of the hazy heat of May;
you loosen it, my love,
that I may wholly see
the beloved boundaries of your body

from Log Dhroim na Gréine to Alt na hUillinne,
from the Malaidh Rua to Mín na hUchta,
below and above, body most beautiful,
every hollow and curve, every sunspot,
every love-spot I'd forgotten

since last I was with you.
I see them again, love, the resplendence
I'd forgotten in the misery of the city.
Oh! don't let me stray again:
Shelter me here between the bright causeway of your legs,
add a fresh dimension to my poem.

translated by Gabriel Fitzmaurice

Níl aon ní, aon ní, a stór,
níos suaimhní ná clapsholas smólaigh
i gCaiseal na gCorr,

ná radharc níos aoibhne
ná buicéad stáin na spéire ag sileadh
solais ar Inis Bó Finne.

Is dá dtiocfá liom, a ghrá,
bheadh briathra ag bláthú ar ghas mo ghutha
mar shiolastrach Ghleann an Átha,

is chluinfeá geantraí sí
i gclingireacht na gcloigíní gorma
i gcoillidh Fhána Bhuí.

Ach b'fhearr leatsa i bhfad
brúchtbhaile balscóideach i mBaile Átha Cliath
lena ghleo tráchta gan stad,

seachas ciúinchónaí sléibhe
mar a gciúnaíonn an ceo le teacht na hoíche
anuas ó Mhín na Craoibhe.

There's nothing, nothing, my love,
more peaceful than a twilight of thrushes
in Caiseal na gCorr,

nor a sight more joyful
than the sky's tin buckets
spilling light on Inis Bó Finne,

and if you would come with me, love,
words would flower on the stem of my voice
like yellow-flag in Gleann an Átha,

and you would hear fairy love-songs
in the tinkle of the bluebells
in the woods of Fána Bhuí.

But you'd much prefer
a smutty suburb in Dublin
with the incessant din of traffic

to the quiet life in the mountain
where the fog falls silent at nightfall
down from Mín na Craoibhe.

translated by Gabriel Fitzmaurice

Do Mhicheál Ó Máirtín

Na portaigh seo i mo thimpeall, thuaidh agus theas
ón tSeascann Mhór amach go hAltán,
bíodh an tionchar céanna acu ar mo dhán
agus atá acu ar an bháchrán —
tugadh siad chun cineáil é le ciúnas.

SILENCE

For Micheál Ó Máirtín

These bogs all round me, north and south
from the *Seascann Mór* on out to *Altán,*
may they effect my poem
as they do the bog-bean —
mature it with silence.

translated by Gabriel Fitzmaurice

Do Pheigí Rose

Teach tréigthe roimhe anocht.
Ar an tairseach, faoi lom na gealaí, nocht,
scáile an tseanchrainn a chuir sé blianta ó shin.

For Peigí Rose

He's back tonight to a deserted house.
On the doorstep, under a brilliant moon, a stark
shadow: the tree he planted years ago is an old tree.

translated by Seamus Heaney

Do Michael Davitt

Anseo ag Stáisiún Chaiseal na gCorr
d'aimsigh mise m'oileán rúin
mo thearmann is mo shanctóir.
Anseo braithim i dtiúin
le mo chinniúint féin is le mo thimpeallacht.
Anseo braithim seasmhacht
is mé ag feiceáil chríocha mo chineáil
thart faoi bhun an Eargail
mar a bhfuil siad ina gcónaí go ciúin
le breis agus trí chéad bliain
ar mhínte féaraigh an tsléibhe
ó Mhín 'a Leá go Mín na Craoibhe.
Anseo, foscailte os mo chomhair
go díreach mar bheadh leabhar ann
tá an taobh tíre seo anois
ó Dhoire Chonaire go Prochlais.
Thíos agus thuas tím na gabháltais
a briseadh as béal an fhiántais.
Seo duanaire mo mhuintire;
an lámhscríbhinn a shaothraigh siad go teann
le dúch a gcuid allais.
Anseo tá achan chuibhreann mar bheadh rann ann
i mórdhán an mhíntíreachais.
Léim anois eipic seo na díograise
i gcanúint ghlas na ngabháltas
is tuigim nach bhfuilim ach ag comhlíonadh dualgais
is mé ag tabhairt dhúshlán an Fholúis
go díreach mar a thug mo dhaoine dúshlán an fhiántais
le dícheall agus le dúthracht
gur thuill siad an duais.

HERE AT CAISEAL NA gCORR STATION

For Michael Davitt

Here at Caiseal na gCorr Station
I discovered my hidden island,
my refuge, my sanctuary.
Here I find myself in tune
with my fate and environment.
Here I feel permanence
as I look at the territory of my people
around the foot of Errigal
where they've settled
for more than three hundred years
on the grassy mountain pastures
from Mín 'a Leá to Mín na Craoibhe.
Here before me, open
like a book,
is this countryside now
from Doire Chonaire to Prochlais.
Above and below, I see the holdings
farmed from the mouth of wilderness.
This is the poem-book of my people,
the manuscript they toiled at
with the ink of their sweat.
Here every enclosed field is like a verse
in the great poem of land reclamation.
I now read this epic of diligence
in the green dialect of the holdings,
understand that I'm only fulfilling my duty
when I challenge the void
exactly as my people challenged the wilderness
with diligence and devotion
till they earned their prize.

Anseo braithim go bhfuil éifeacht i bhfilíocht.
Braithim go bhfuil brí agus tábhacht liom mar dhuine
is mé ag feidhmiú mar chuisle de chroí mo chine
agus as an chinnteacht sin tagann suaimhneas aigne.
Ceansaítear mo mhianta, séimhítear mo smaointe,
cealaítear contrárthachtaí ar an phointe.

Here I feel the worth of poetry.
I feel my *raison d'être* and importance as a person
as I become the pulse of my people's heart
and from this certainty comes peace of mind.
My desires are tamed, my thoughts mellow,
contradictions are cancelled on the spot.

translated by Gabriel Fitzmaurice

FOTHRACH TÍ I MÍN NA CRAOIBHE

Do Noel Ó Gallchóir

Tá creatlach an tseantí
ag baint ceoil as an ghaoth;
gan doras gan fuinneog gan sclátaí dín
gach foscailt ina feadóg fhiáin
ag gabháil fhoinn.

Ó bhinn go binn
tá an teach tréighe éirithe
ina shiansa stoirmspreagtha.
Mo cheol thú, a sheantí;
a leithéid de phortaíocht
ní chluinfí choíche
ó theach téagartha teaghlaigh
lá gaoithe.

RUIN OF HOUSE IN MÍN NA CRAOIBHE

For Noel Ó Gallchóir

The old house, with skeletal grace,
is making music of the wind.
Without door or window
or the shelter of slates,
every wound is a tin-whistle
making wild music.

From gable to gable
the exhausted house rises
into a storm-melody.
Such music, old house!
The likes of your lilting
has never been heard
on any windy day
in a comfortable, domestic place.

translated by Thomas McCarthy

IDIR MÁM AN tSEANTÍ AGUS
LOCH NA mBREAC BEADAÍ

Anseo, díreach anseo, a chroí,
i measc na dtortóg fraoigh, fág síos mé;
fág síos mé le turnamh an lae
agus cuirfidh tú sonrú sna seangáin
a bheas ag caolú leo go righin réidh
as mo shúile cinn
agus grian mhullach an Chairn
á dtreorú lena cuid gealán —
ach ná bíodh aon scanradh ort go deo
faoin taispeánadh aduain seo;
mo bheatha a bheas ann, a ghrá,
mo bheatha ag bogadh go buach
go cónaí éigin nua.

BETWEEN *MÁM AN tSEANTÍ* AND *LOCH NA mBREAC BEADAÍ*

Here, right here, my love,
Among the heather-mounds, lay me down,
Lay me down as day declines
And you'll see the ants
Edging relentlessly
From my eyes
As the sun on the top of *Carn Traona*
Guides them with its light;
But don't be frightened
Of this eerie sight:
My life 'twill be, love,
My life triumphantly
Moving house.

translated by Gabriel Fitzmaurice

Bailc shamhraidh sna cnoic —
i dtitim throm thréan na fearthainne
cloisim míle bó bhainne á mblí.

I mbáine an gheimhridh sna cnoic
bíonn na bunsoip trom le sioc —
as a gcuid siní sileann tost.

A heavy summer shower in the hills —
In the teeming downpour,
I hear a thousand cows being milked.

In the winter whiteness of the hills
thatch-eaves are heavy with frost —
from their teats, silence drips.

translated by Cathal Ó Searcaigh

SCUAINE

Do Valerie Lynch

Ó Mhín na Craoibhe go Gort a' Choirce
tá an gleann seo órnite
tar éis maidin de sciúradh gréine.

Ar ball, le gach aon séideog chráite
beidh scuaine de thaiscéalaithe saoire
chugainn ar lorg órghréine.

SUNRUSH

For Valerie Lynch

From *Mín na Craoibhe* to *Gort a' Choirce*
The glen gleams in a wash of gold
Scoured by the sun since morning.

Now the struggling wheezers come —
Sunday conquistadores —
Staking their share of the sun!

translated by Gabriel Rosenstock

Do Ann Craig

Corraím as mo chodladh i dtoibinne
maidin chruaidh gheimhridh
is trí fhuinneoigín na seanchistine
tím splanc dhearg an choiligh
ag bladhmadh isteach ar mo leabaidh
ag leá as mo shúile, braoinín
ar bhraoinín, biríní siocáin an tsuain
maidin i Mín 'a Leá.

Ó bhaitheas go bonn, bogaim le teocht
is altaím le méid mo bhuíochais
an glaochsholas a leánn domhsa ar a seacht
siocfhuacht an dorchadais:
óir, asat, a mheall chíríneach a thagann
i ndúlaíocht an gheimhridh
léas tosaigh an lae
maidin i Mín 'a Leá.

Ar leisciúlacht aigne is láimhe
fógraíonn tú críoch
le caor thine do theachtaireachta.
Sleamhnaím anois as mo tháimhe
ar nós maidhm shneachta
anuas malaidh chrochta na leapa
chuig gealadh an lae
maidin i Mín 'a Leá.

MORNING IN MÍN 'A LEÁ

For Ann Craig

I start suddenly from my sleep
this hard winter's morning
and through the little window of the kitchen
I see the red flash of the rooster
lighting up my bed,
melting from my eyes, drop
by drop, the icicles of sleep
this morning in Mín 'a Leá.

From head to foot, I soften with heat
and with all the thanks I can
I praise this morning call of light that comes at seven
to melt the frozen cold of dark,
for from you, you with your crested orb,
comes, in these dark depths of winter,
the first gleam of dawn,
this morning in Mín 'a Leá.

You proclaim the demise
of deadmindedness and sloth
with the fireball of your message.
I slide now from my lethargy
like an avalanche
down the brow of the bed
to daybreak
this morning in Mín 'a Leá.

translated by Gabriel Fitzmaurice

tar éis eadra
thosaigh crainn ag síothlú na gaoithe

de rúid reatha
anuas an tArd, phreab carraigeacha

ina gcait chraosacha

After morning milking-time
the trees began to strain the wind

when, with a rush running
down from the height, rocks pounced

hunger-crazed cats.

translated by Cathal Ó Searcaigh

HAIKÚ

Do Mháirín Ní Dhubhchoin

Speal mo sheanathar
ag meirgiú sa scíoból —
clapsholas Fómhair

Dritheog nó dhó fágtha
I mbucóid luatha an tseanduine —
grian na glasmhaidine.

Gealach na gcoinleach —
tá úll dearg san fhuinneog
is an dath ag siothlú as

(I mo sheomra leapa)

Oiche fhada gheimhridh —
cumhaidh ar an chuileog fosta
léi féin sa leabaidh

For Máirín Ní Dhubhchoin

My grandfather's scythe
Rusting in the barn —
harvest twilight

translated by Gabriel Fitzmaurice.

An ember or two glow
in the old man's ash bucket —
Winter morning sun

Harvest moon —
As red fades from the apple
Set in the window

(In my bedroom)

Long Winter's night —
the fly grieves too
alone in the bed.

translated by Gréagóir Ó Dúill

Do Sheosamh Watson

Oícheanta geimhridh agus muid ag cuartaíocht
i dtigh Neddie Eoin i mbarr na Míne Buí
bhíodh seanchiteal súicheach ag portaíocht
ar an chrochadh os cionn na tineadh
ag coinneáil ceoil le seit na mbladháirí
a dhamsaigh thart i dteallach na cisteanadh.

Bhíodh gaotha na gcnoc ag trupáil fán tairseach
amhail buachaillí bradacha nach ligfí isteach
agus muidne le mugaí móra galach le tae
'nár suí go sochmaidh os comhair an tseanchaí;
drithleoga dearga a bhriathra ina spréacha
ag lasadh na samhlaíocht' ionainn go réidh.

Agus é ag drithliú ansiúd ina choirneál scéalaíochta
bhíodh muidne ag airneál fá chlúdaigh a aigne,
ag tabhairt rúscadh na gríosaí dá chuimhne
amanta le ceisteanna casta ár bhfiosrachta
agus é ag eachtraíocht fána shaol ar an Lagán
agus ar fheirmeacha East Lothian na hAlban.

Bhíodh a ghlór chomh teolaí le tinigh smután, lán
de shiosán agus de shrann agus é ag spalpadh
dáin de chuid Bhurns dúinn ó thús go deireadh —
'Tam O' Shanter' nó b'fhéidir 'Kellyburn Braes'
agus chomh luath agus a chanadh sé 'Scots Wha Hae'
tchífeá bladhairí ag splancarnaigh as a shúile.

For Seosamh Watson

Winter nights when we rambled
to Neddie Eoin's at the top of *Mín Bhuí*
A sooty old kettle lilted
on the hook above the fire
keeping time with the flames
as they danced a set on the hearth.

Hill winds clattered on the threshold
— blackguards who weren't let in —
while we composed ourselves, mugs of tea steaming in our hands,
as we sat before the storyteller,
the red sparks of his words spluttering
to life in our imaginations.

While he crackled with stories there in his corner
we'd explore the fire-place of his mind
stirring the embers of his memory
with the vexed questions of our curiosity,
as he'd hold us with yarns of the Lagan
and about the farms of East Lothian in Scotland.

His voice was warm as a bogwood fire
hissing and soughing as he
rattled off one of Burns' poems from start to finish —
'Tam O' Shanter' or maybe*'Kellyburn Braes'*
and as soon as he struck up*'Scots Wha Hae'*
you'd see the flames flashing in his eyes.

Bhíodh siollaí gaile ag éirí as a phíopa cré
agus é ag trácht ar mharcraí buile Ailigh
a mhúsclós maidin inteacht le deargadh an lae
le hÉirinn a chosaint i gCogadh an Dá Rí,
is bhíodh muidne ag marcaíocht ar sheanstól bhuí
ag tapú ina n-araicis i mBearna na Mucaise.

Is bhíodh muidne ag seilg bídh leis na Fianna
ó Oirthear Dhumhaigh go barr na Beithí,
is ag imirt cnaige le curaidh na hEamhna
ar na méilte féaraigh i Machaire Rabhartaigh;
is chonaic muid an slua sí oíche Shamhna
ag siamsaíocht ar bhealach Fhána Bhuí.

Ó ba mhéanar a bheith arís ag cuartaíocht
na hoícheanta geimhridh seo i dtigh Neddie Eoin,
mo ghoradh féin ar a dheismireacht bhéil
agus é ag baint lasadh asam lena mholadh;
gach focal ina aibhleog dhearg ag spréachadh
chugam go teolaí as tinidh chroíúil a scéil.

Tá sé corradh le fiche bliain anois
ó chuaigh a thinidh as, i mbarr na Míne Buí
ach istigh anseo i gcoigilt mo chuimhne
drithlíonn beo nó dhó den tinidh adaí
is leáfaidh na drithleoga sin an dubhacht
a mhothaím anocht i bhféitheoga an chroí.

Smoke syllables rose from his clay pipe
when he drew down the mad horseman of *Aileach*
who'll resurrect some morning at daybreak
to defend Ireland in the War of the Two Kings
while we rode the old yellowstool
galloping to meet them in Muckish Gap.

And we hunted food with the Fianna
from *Oirthear Dhumhaigh* to the top of *Beithí*
 played hurling with the heroes of *Eamhain*
on the grassy dunes of *Machaire Rabhartaigh,*
and saw the Otherworld on hallowe'en night
sporting on the road to *Fana Bhuí.*

Oh how I'd love to ramble again
these Winter nights to Neddie Eoin's,
to warm myself in the spell of his talk,
blushing in his praise —
each word a red hot coal firing
me from the hearty glow of his story.

His fire is out these twenty years
or more at the top of *Mín Bhuí*
but here in the banked hearth of my memory
a live coal or two from that fire sparkles,
and those sparks will dissolve the gloom
I feel in my heart tonight.

translated by Gabriel Fitzmaurice.

Do Bhríd, Maighread agus Sorcha

Bhí féith na feola inti ach fosta féith an ghrinn
agus in ainneoin go raibh sí mantach agus mórmhionnach
ní raibh sí riamh gruama nó grusach linn
nuair a bhíodh sinn thuas aici ar an Domhnach,
is dhéanadh sí splais tae dúinn os cionn na gríosaí,
is í ag cur spleoid ar seo, is spréadh ar siúd go teasaí.

Is ba mhinic í ag gearán fán *tseanbhugger* de *ghauger*
a ghearr siar í sa phinsean is a d'fhág í ar an bheagán
cionn is go raibh bó i mbéal beirthe aici sa bhóitheach
cúpla bearach ar féarach agus dornán caorach
agus í ag trácht ar an eachtra deireadh sí go feargach:
"Sa tír seo tugtar na *crusts* is cruaidhe don té atá mantach."

Is chuidíodh muid léi i dtólamh ar an Domhnach
aoileach na seachtaine a chartadh as an bhóitheach,
is nuair a bhíodh muid ag déanamh faillí inár ngnaithe,
ag bobaireacht ar chúl a cinn is ag broimnigh,
deireadh sí, "Á cuirigí séip oraibh féin a chailleacha,
ní leasóidh broim an talamh san earrach."

" Bhfuil *jizz* ar bith ionaibh, a bhuachaillí?" a deireadh sí
nuair a bhíodh leisc orainn easaontú lena tuairimí.
"Oró tá sibh chomh bómánta le huain óga an earraigh,
ach sin an rud atá na sagairt is na TD's a iarraidh,
is nuair a thiocfas sibhse i méadaíocht, a bhuachaillí,
ní bheidh moill ar bith orthu sibh a thiomáint mar chaoirigh."

Chothaigh sí í féin ansiúd mar a dhéanfadh crann
ag feo is ag fás de réir an tséasúir a bhí ann.

116

MOUNTAIN WOMAN

For Bríd, Maighread and Sorcha

She inclined to flesh but also to fun
And though she was fond of swearing and gap-toothed
She was never gruff or gloomy with us
When we visited her on Sundays
And she made us a drop of tea
While she hotly 'dashed' this and 'dratted' that.

Often she complained of the "oul' bugger of a gauger"
Who had cut her back in the pension and who had left her with little
because she had a cow about to calve in the byre
a few heifers grazing and a handful of sheep
and when she referred to the event she'd say angrily
"In this country the hardest crusts are given to those with least teeth."

And we always helped her on Sundays
to muck out the week's dung from the byre.
And when we neglected our work
playacting and farting behind her back
she'd say "Ah! lads! would you put a shape on yourselves,
a fart won't fertilise the farm in Spring.'

'Have you any jizz at all in you boys,' she'd say,
when we were embarrassed to disagree with her.
'Arrah, you are as stupid as young spring lambs,
But that's what the priests and the T.D's want
and when you grow up, boys,
they'll have no trouble driving you like sheep.

She kept herself there like a tree
growing and withering according to the season

"Ní ag aoisiú atá mé," a deireadh sí "ach ag apú,"
is mar shíolta thitfeadh a briathra in úir mhéith m'aigne
is nuair a shnaidhmeadh sí a géaga thart orm go teann
mhothaínn an gheir — fáinní fáis a colainne.

"Níl crann sna flaithis níos airde na Crann na Foighde"
a deireadh sí agus í ag foighneamh go fulangach leis an bhás
a bhí ag lomadh agus ag creachadh a géaga gan spás.
Anois cuirim Aifreann lena hanam ó am go ham i gcuimhne
ar an toradh a bhronn sí orm ó Chrann na hAithne
agus mar a déarfadh sí féin dá mbeadh sí ina beathaidh,

"Is fearr cogar sa chúirt ná scread ar an tsliabh, a thaiscidh."

"It's not ageing I am, but ripening,"
and her words fell like seeds into the welcoming earth of my mind.
And when she'd wrap me in her limbs so tightly,
I felt the fat — the growth rings of her body.

"Patience is the highest tree in heaven,"
She'd say while she patiently endured the approach of death
which robbed and stripped her limbs without cease.
Now and again I have a Mass said for her in memory
of the fruit she bestowed on me from the Tree of Knowledge
and because, as she'd say herself if she were alive,

"A murmur in court beats a roar on the moor, my dear."

translated by Lillis Ó Laoire

Do Liam Ó Coinneagáin

I mbathlach ceann slinne a chaith sé a shaol
leath bealaigh i gcoinne Chnoc an tSéideáin;
drúncaire, a raibh a dhreach is a dheilbh maol
agus lomchnámhach, macasamhail an screabáin
ina thimpeall, áit a bhfuarthas marbh é anuraidh
caite sa scrobarnach, lá polltach geimhridh:
a naoi mbliana fichead múchta ag ainíde dí,
is gan glór lena chaoineadh ach gocarsach cearc fraoigh.

Inniu, bhí fear an tsolais thuas ar bharr an tsímléara
ag scoitheadh sreanga leictreach. "Tá'n bás," ar seisean,
agus é ag meabhrú ar bhás anabaí an úinéara,
"dálta gearradh cumhachta. Ainneoin ár dtola a thig sé
de ghnáth. Ach an té a dhéanann faillí i bhfiacha an tsolais
a thiarcais, nach é féin cúis a dhorchadais."

THE E.S.B. BILL

For Liam Ó Coinneagáin

In a slated cabin he spent his life,
half-way along the Hill of the Winds.
A drunk, his face and gait had the rough
and bare-boned character of scrub, of whins.
It was there he was found only last year,
emptied of life in the piercing winter;
his twenty-nine years drenched in beer —
his lament, a grouse's clucking despair.

Today the ESB man was at the chimney,
disconnecting the supply. 'Death,' he said,
(thinking of the young man so recently dead)
'death is like being cut off by the ESB —
the man who lets all his bills go unpaid
has already known the darkness of the dead."

translated by Thomas McCarthy.

Do Ghréagóir Ó Dúill

Ina chrága cranracha, ina shiúl spadánta
tá trí scór bliain de chruacht agus de chruatan,
de choraíocht bhuan le talamh tíoránta
an tsléibhe, ansiúd os cionn Loch Altáin.
Talamh gortach gann a d'ól le blianta
allas a dhíograise is a d'fhág é chomh spíonta,
chomh lomchnámhach le stumpán caoráin.
Agus na mianta a bhláthaigh i bhfearann a chroí
shearg siad go tapaidh de dhíobháil solais
i bProchlais iargúlta i mbéal an uaignis
san áit nach dtig aoibh ar an spéir ach go hannamh
is nach ndéanann an ghrian ach corrdhraothadh.

Ansiúd faoi scáth arrachtach an tsléibhe
níor aoibhnigh bean é le fuiseoga a póg
is níor neadaigh suáilcí an ghrá
aon lá riamh i bhfiántas a chléibhe.
Tá siúl an tsléibhe ag a thréad beag caorach
ó abhainn Mhín an Mhadaidh go barr na Beithí
ach tá sé teanntaithe é féin ó bhí sé ina stócach
ag na claíocha críche atá thart air go bagrach
ach amháin nuair bhíonn braon beag imithe chun a chinn.
Ansin éalaíonn a smaointe as raon a intleachta
mar chaoirigh siúlacha in ocras an gheimhridh
ag cuartú féaraigh i ndiamhra an tsléibhe.

Ansiúd is minic creathnú an bháis ina chroí
nuair a tí sé cnáfairt chnámh ina shlí
nó a chuid madadh ag coscairt conablaigh
sna cnoic adaí atá lán de chiúnas agus de chaoirigh.

122

SHEPHERD

For Gréagóir Ó Dúill

In his calloused hands, in his sluggish gait
there are sixty years of hardness and hardship,
of constant struggle with the tyranny of the mountain
there above Loch Altán.
Hungry, mean land that for years drained
 the sweat of his fervour and left him spent
and skeletal as a bog-stump.
And the desires that flowered in his heart's fields
withered quickly for want of light
in remote Prochlais in the mouth of the wilderness
where the sky but seldom smiles,
the sun laughs only the odd wry laugh.

Here in the monstrous shadow of the mountain
no woman ever pleasured him with the larks of her kisses,
the joys of love never nested
in the wilderness of his heart.
His little flock of sheep have the run of the mountain
from Mín an Mhadaidh river to the top of Beithigh
but he is bound since youth
to the boundary ditches that surround him, menacing
except when the wee drop's gone to his head.
Then his thoughts escape the beaten track of intellect —
wandering sheep in the hunger of winter
seeking grazing in dark mountain recesses.

There horror of death often trembles in his heart
when he sees skeletons on the path
or his dogs tearing carcasses
in hills pregnant with silence and sheep.

Agus dála gheir rósta na muiceola is na feola
a bheir tinneas bhéal an ghoile dó gach lá
luíonn an dorchadas go trom ar a aigne —
an dorchadas a ramhraíonn anuas ón Achla
le teacht na hoíche is a líonann é le heagla.

Ansiúd san oíche ina chisteanach lom leacach,
cruptha ina chathaoir os comhair na tineadh,
bíonn sé ag humáil is ag hútháil faoina anáil
leis an uaigneas a choinneáil ó dhoras, an t-uafás
a bhíonn ag drannadh leis as an dorchadas
is a shleamhnódh chuige isteach ach faill a fháil
le creach a dhéanamh ina chloigeann,
go díreach mar a ní na luchógaí móra
crúbáil is creimseáil os a chionn ar an tsíleáil.

Fadó bhíodh a chroí ag bualadh le bród
nuair a bhíodh an Druma Mór ag teacht ar an fhód
go bríomhar buacach, Lá Fhéil' Pádraig ar an Fhál Charrach.
Oícheantaí anois agus é ina luí ar a leabaidh
cluineann sé druma maolaithe a sheanchroí
ag gabháil in ísle brí agus ag éirí stadach. . .

And just as the dripping of bacon and roast-meat
give him indigestion daily,
the dark lies heavy on his mind —
the dark which thickens down from Achla
at nightfall and terrifies him.

There at night in his bare, flag-floored kitchen
hunched in his chair before the fire
he hums and haws sotto voce
to keep the loneliness from his door, the terror
which snarls at him from the night
which would sneak in given half a chance
to prey upon his mind
just as the rats
claw and nibble at the ceiling above him.

Long ago his heart beat with pride
when the Big Drum paraded
lively and proud on Saint Patrick's Day in Falcarragh.
Nights now in bed
he hears his old heart's muffled drum
growing weaker and faltering ...

translated by Gabriel Fitzmaurice

Do Liam Ó Muirthile

D'éirigh sé dúthuirseach déarfainn
den uaigneas a shníonn anuas i dtólamh
fríd na maolchnocáin is fríd na gleanntáin
chomh malltriallach le *hearse* tórraimh;
de bhailte beaga marbhánta na mbunchnoc
nach bhfuil aos óg iontu ach oiread le créafóg;
de na seanlaochra, de lucht roiste na dtortóg
a d'iompaigh an domasach ina deargfhód
is a bhodhraigh é *pink* bliain i ndiaidh bliana
ag éisteacht leo ag maíomh as seanfhóid an tseantsaoil;

de na *bungalows* bheaga bhána atá chomh gránna
le *dandruff* in ascaill chíbeach an Ghleanna;
de na daoine óga gafa i g*cage* a gcinniúna
dálta ainmhithe allta a chaill a ngliceas;
de thrí thrua na scéalaíochta i dtruacántas
lucht na dífhostaíochta, den easpa meanmna,
den iargúltacht, den chúngaigeantacht ar dhá thaobh an Ghleanna;
de na leadhbacha breátha thíos i dTigh Ruairí
a chuir an fear ag bogadaigh ann le fonn
ach nach dtabharfadh túrálú ar a raibh de shú ann;

de theorainneacha treibhe, de sheanchlaíocha teaghlaigh,
de bheith ag mún a mhíshástachta in éadan na mballaí
a thóg cine agus creideamh thart air go teann.
D'éirigh sé dúthuirseach de bheith teanntaithe sa Ghleann
is le rúide bó bradaí maidin amháin earraigh
chlearáil sé na ballaí is *hightailáil* anonn adaí.

126

A BRADDY COW

For Liam Ó Muirthile

He got fed-up, I'd swear,
of the loneliness that constantly seeps down,
through the rolling hills, through the valleys
sluggish as a hearse;
of the lazy hamlets of the foothills
empty of youth as of earth;
of the old warriors, of the sodbusters
who turned to red-sod the peaty soil
and who deafened him pink, year-in, year-out,
bragging of the old sods of the past;

of the small, white bungalows ugly
as dandruff in the sedgy headlands of the Glen;
of the young trapped in the cage of their fate
like wild animals who have lost their cunning;
of the three sorrows of storytelling in the misery
of the unemployed, of low spirits,
of the backwardness, of the narrowmindedness of both sides of the Glen,
of the fine birds below in Ruairí's
who stirred the man in him
but who couldn't care less about his lusting;

of tribal boundaries, of ancient household ditches,
of pissing his frustration at race and religion
that walled him in.
He got fed up of being fettered in the Glen
and, bucking like a braddy cow one spring morning,
he cleared the walls and hightailed away.

translated by Gabriel Fitzmaurice

Do Mary agus Danny Cannon

Na crucairt mar mhanaigh
ag cantaireacht sa chlúdaigh
agus seanchiteal cráifeach
ag monabhracht faoina anáil
os cionn na gríosaí
agus Neddie, dea-mhéineach
agus diaganta ina chathaor cois teallaigh —
Halo tobac fá dhealramh a dhreacha —
ag praeitseáil dúinne
cuairteoirí beaga an Domhnaigh
ceachtanna croíúla
as leabhar beo a bheatha
agus sna soiscéalta tíriúla
idir smailceanna smaointeacha dá phíopa
ag meabhrú dúinn go rógánta
cá bith fá rud ar bith
gan dóigh a dhéanamh dár mbarúil.

Agus muidinne, na pleidhcí beaga ainglí
a dhealraigh le Dia
an seanmháistir gnaíúil adaí,
chan ábhar iontais anois, b'fhéidir,
agus mé in aois fir
go ndeirim rudaí nach bhfuil sa Phaidir.

CREED

For Mary and Danny Cannon

The crickets like monks
chanting at the chimney corner
and a devout old kettle
murmuring under its breath
above the glowing embers
and Neddie, benevolent
and godly in his fireside chair —
his features resplendent in their Halo of tobacco —
preaching to us
the little Sunday visitors
hearty lessons
from the living book of his life
and in the homely gospels
between thoughtful puffs of his pipe
reminding us impishly
whatever about anything
not to become trapped by our opinions.

And we, the angelic little rascals
who likened to God
that pleasant old master,
it is no wonder now, perhaps,
as a man,
that I say things which are not in the Lord's Prayer.

translated by Lillis Ó Laoire

129

Do Chiarán agus Fiona

"Is bráithre muid go léir,"
arsa an manach le m'athair
ach nuair a thrasnaíos
an cur i gcéill go groí
le "macasamhail Cháin is Aibéil"
chreathnaíos. Bhí miodóga
fionaíolacha na súl
sáite ionam go croí.

For Ciarán and Fiona

'We are all brothers,"
the monk said to my father.
but when I countered
his flattering cliché —
'like Cain and Abel'

I had to shiver.
The fratricidal dagger of his stare
was deep in my breast.

translated by Thomas McCarthy

SCRÚDÚ COINSIASA
ROIMH DHUL CHUN SUAIN

Do Phil Ó Connor

Faic na fríde de bhraodar
níor chuir d'anbhás, a thraonaigh,
ar thiománaí an innill bhainte.
Bhí aoibh go dtí na cluasa air
is an roth ag gabháil tharat.
"Argentina attacking," ar seisean,
ag strácáil do choirp lena chosa
is i snapchasadh amháin
bhuail sé urchar de chic ort
isteach i mbearna sa chlaí.

Níor dhúirt mé "sea" nó "ní hea".
"Is beag an díobháil a ní béal druidte",
a hoileadh domh le blianta.
'Dhia! Is mé is suaraí amuigh. Féach
cáil mo mhacántachta
á caitheamh agam os comhair cháich
dálta thodóg Havana
agus toisc faichill mo thóna féin
a bheith orm, tá riar a cháis
á choinneáil agam le gach caime.

Ó, a thraonaigh,
tá'n tost ag cur do thuairisc' anocht
is i measc na ndoilíos
ar mhéanar domhsa a dhearmad
anois gan sonrú

cuimhním ort.

EXAMINATION OF CONSCIENCE
BEFORE GOING TO BED

For Phil O Connor

He was in his element,
the mowing machine driver,
his face slit in a murderous grin
as the wheel went over you.
"Argentina attacking" he offered
dragging your corpse out
then, cocking his boot like a pistol,
he blasted you into the ditch.

I said nothing.
"A shut mouth does little harm" —
one lesson well learned.
God, I'm a poor specimen.
I suck on my honest name
like a fat Havana
and look out for myself. See, I'm not afraid
to be implicated ...

Still, my mown-down corncrake,
the silence asks for you tonight
and among the griefs
I don't mind forgetting
now, vaguely,

I remember you.

translated by Peter Sirr

Do Sheosamh Ó Dubhchoin

Hiúdaí agus Padaí, pinsinéirí na Ceathrúna,
chuala mé iad Aoine amháin Samhna
taobh amuigh d'oifig phoist Ghort an Choirce
ag caint ar an chostas maireachtála
a bhí ina chúis broide acu achan lá ·
is a bhí ag dul i ndéine is i ndéine
mar an brú fola is an saothar anála.

"Tá'n tír seo ar maos i gcac, a Phadaí,"
arsa Hiúdaí, a shúil ar an pheata madaidh
a d'fhág práib chaca i lár an bhealaigh.
"Agus ar an *ghovernment* atá an locht.
Tá siad ag cac orainn, maidin agus tráthnóna,
scút de bhréaga agus de bhéal bocht
ag *deny*áil go bhfuil orthu féin poll tóna."

"*Galoots!* Sin a bhfuil iontu," arsa Padaí.
"Ach inniu tá traidhfil puntaí inár bpócaí
thig linn an saol a ghlacadh go réidh.
An cuimhneach leat am an *free beef?* "
Nocht grian dhalltach ina gcoinne
is chonaic mé a gcaipíní is a gcuimhní
á ligean anuas acu diaidh ar ndiaidh,

lena súile a chosaint ar sholas scéiniúil an lae.

THE COLLOQUY OF THE ANCIENTS

For Seosamh Ó Dubhchoin

Hiúdaí and Paddy, the pensioners from Keeldrum,
I heard them on an All-Souls Friday
Outside Gortahork Post Office
Musing on the price of living
Which was a wild bother to them every day
And only getting worse and worse
Like blood pressure and the gasping breath.

"This country's sunk in shite, Paddy,"
Said Hiúdaí, his eye on the pet dog
Who'd dropped a load in the middle of the road.
"And the government's to blame,
They're shiteing on us, morn till eve,
Big lumps of lies, and their own poor mouths
Denying an arsehole in themselves."

"Galoots is all they are!," said Paddy.
"But today, a pound or two in our pockets
We'll tackle life with midlin' ease.
Do you mind the time the beef was free?"
The sun blinded all before them
And I saw their caps and memories
Being leisurely tugged down,

To guard their eyes from incandescent day.

translated ny Frank Galligan

135

Do Thomás Mac Giolla Bhríde

Ansiúd i gceartlár charn an aoiligh
atá an crann róis ag fás.
Tá an boladh bréan ar gach taobh dó
chomh maith leis an bhrocamas
a chartar amach le haoileach na bó;
rudaí raiceáilte atá imithe ó mhaitheas,
brat staighre stróicthe, forc aon bheangán,
seanscáthán craiceáilte, stól corrach;
Iad clampáilte thart air go teann, slabhraí
a bhrúnn as a ghéaga an súlach
agus i gcónaí bíonn sciotar an eallaigh
splaiseáilte ar a chabhail;
agus bíonn glamanna gáifeacha gaoithe
ag glúrascnaigh fríd mar dhiabhail.

Ach ní chuireann an truailliú ná an tuairteáil
beaguchtach ar bith ar an róschrann.
Beag beann ar mhiodamas, beag beann ar dhíobháil,
ar neamhchead gach braighdeáin,
nochtann seisean do ghrian an tsamhraidh
cumhracht dhearg a chroí
agus bronnann sé mil go fial ar bheacha
i gcomhair an gheimhridh.

Macasamhail an chrainn seo, a Mhiley,
fáisceadh tusa as saol a bhí dian
agus is é do chinniúint riamh ó shin
bheith beo i mbroid agus i bpian,
ach is ainneoin gach mí-áidh agus smoladh,
aoibhníonn tusa sa tsamhradh

136

For Tomás Mac Giolla Bhríde

Beyond in the core of the midden,
There is a rose-tree growing.
On either side, the fetor hangs
Around the waste
Cleared out with the dung of the cows:
A torn stair-carpet, a one pronged fork,
An old cracked mirror, a shaky stool;
All clamped tightly around her — chains
That squeeze the sap from her limbs;
The skitter of the cattle forever
Splashing on her stem;
And a frenzied baying wind
Howling like the devil about her.

But neither trash nor tempest
Is a bother to the rose.
Little *meas* on dung or deprivation.
Despite the tentacles that bind her
She flashes at the summer sun,
The red succulence of her heart
And to the bees her honeyed breasts
To keep them for the winter.

As it is with her, Miley,
You too rose from life's hard wasteground,
And you are damned ever since
To grow in suffering and in pain,
But despite the blight and misfortune,
You blossom come the summer

agus bíonn do bhriathra ina mblátha fáin
ag cumhrú an tí le bríomhaireacht.
Tigimse ag tóraíocht meala, lón anama,
a thaiscím i gcoirceog mo dháin.

And like the flowers that love to stray,
Your words are fragrance about the house.
I come in search of honey, soul food,
Secreted in the labyrinth of my lines.

translated by Frank Galligan

A cheann dubh dílis dílis dílis
d'fhoscail ár bpóga créachtaí Chríosta arís;
ach ná foscail do bhéal, ná sceith uait an scéal:
tá ár ngrá ar an taobh thuathal den tsoiscéal.

Tá cailíní na háite seo cráite agat, a ghrá,
's iad ag iarraidh thú a bhréagadh is a mhealladh gach lá;
ach b'fhearr leatsa bheith liomsa i mbéal an uaignis
'mo phógadh, 'mo chuachadh is mo thabhairt chun aoibhnis.

Is leag do cheann dílis dílis dílis,
leag do cheann dílis i m'ucht a dhíograis;
ní fhosclód mo bhéal, ní sceithfead an scéal
ar do shonsa shéanfainn gach soiscéal.

My blackhaired love, my dear, dear, dear,
Our kiss re-opens Christ's wounds here;
But close your mouth, don't spread the word:
We offend the Gospels with our love.

You plague the local belles, my sweet,
They attempt to coax you with deceit
But you'd prefer my lonely kiss,
You hugging me to bring to bliss.

Lay your head my dear, dear, dear,
Lay your head on my breast here;
I'll close my mouth, no detail break —
I'd deny the Gospels for your sake.

translated by Gabriel Fitzmaurice

Tá mé ag síorshiúl sléibhe ar feadh na hoíche
ó Mhalaidh na Gaoithe suas go barr Mhín na Craoibhe
is ó thréig tú aréir mé — cé shamhlódh é choíche —
tá mo shaolsa níos loime na blár seo an tsléibhe.

Chiap tú mé is chráigh tú mé is d'fhág tú mar seo mé
gan romham is gan i mo dhiaidh ach seachrán agus sliabh,
gan amach i ndán domh as duibheagán seo an dorchadais,
óir ba tusa an ball bán a bhí riamh ar an oíche i mo chliabh.

Bhéarfainnse a bhfuil agam agus flaitheas Dé lena chois
ach mé a bheith sínte anois idir tusa agus saol na ngeas.
Ó, a cheann dea-chumtha agus a chorp na háilleachta,
b'fhearr amharc amháin ort anocht ná solas síoraí na bhFlaitheas.

WANDERING THE MOUNTAINSIDE

I am wandering the mountainside all night long and grieving
From Malaidh na Gaoithe to the top of Mín na Craoibhe,
Since last night you left me — oh most unhappy chance —
My life is barer than this mountainous expanse.

You tormented and distressed me and left me in the lurch,
Nought before and nought behind me but mountain and my search,
Nothing before me now or ever but night's abyss, this dark
For you were the one bright spot in the midnight of my heart.

I'd offer my possessions and all of Heaven too
To be stretched between my loved one and the world of taboo.
O lovely head and body, I'd prefer one single sight
Of you this night than Heaven, than everlasting light.

translated by Gabriel Fitzmaurice

Tá mo chéadsearc i Londain le bliain agus trí ráithe,
Ach focal beag ná scéala char sheol sé thar sáile.
Tá a sheoladh ar mo theangaidh is a ainm i mbéal mo chléibhe
Ach go gcuirfidh sé mo thuairisc cha bhíonn ach tost ó na sléibhte.

Inniu is mé ag siúl mar a dtéimis i gcónaí Dé Domhnaigh
Suas Malaidh na Míne is amach droim Loch an Ghainimh,
Bhí cuma bheag chaillte ar sheanbhailte bánaithe na gcnoc
Is a hoiread leo siúd, ó d'imigh tú uaim, níl gnaoi ar mo shaol.

I mo luí domh, i mo shuí domh, i mo sheasamh nó i mo shuan,
A bhuachaill an chinn chataigh, cuimhním ort go buan
Óir ba tusa an lámh ba shéimhe a leag méar orm ariamh
Is ó d'imigh tú, tá talamh méith m'aigne ag tiontú aríst 'na shliabh.

Cion istigh a bheith agam duit is cion amuigh a d'fhág mise ar an bhfaraoir
Is tú anois i bhfad ó láimh is gan fonn ort bheith i mo ghaobhair;
Chan bris duit mo bhuairt is chan buaireamh duit mo phian
Is mar barr ar an donas b'fhéidir gur cuma leat, a mhian.

Mar an ghealach sin a shleamhnaigh isteach fuinneog an dín
Is a ghoid codladh na hoíche uaim ó mo leabaidh shuain,
Aniar aduaidh a tháinig an grá orm, aniar aduaidh is isteach i mo chroí,
Is é a sciob uaim mo stuaim is a d'fhág folamh mé choíche.

TO MY HEART'S DESIRE IN LONDON

My love is in London three seasons and a year
But no little whisper has come over from that land,
My heart knows his name and tells it to my ear
And the mountains stay mute and pretend to understand.

Today, like all Sundays, I'm out taking the air,
Up by Malaidh na Míne, way beyond the Sandy Lake,
The villages are all empty, windswept and bare
As though they had died in their sleep for your sake.

As I lie, as I sit — awake or asleep —
Your curls torment me, deep deep inside,
As I think of your soft fingers, deep in me, deep
I know that a landscape has withered and died.

My secret desire that I failed to conceal!
And now you're in London, far from my gaze:
What the eye cannot see the heart cannot feel
And will you ignore me the rest of your days?

Like the moon that is furtively paling my room
Stealing my dreams and keeping me awake,
Love came from afar, from a distant gloom
And shimmered awhile like one cloud on a lake.

translated by Gabriel Rosenstock.

Dúirt tú liom agus tú ag imeacht
Gan d'ainm a lua níos mó ....

Agus rinne mé mar a dúirt tú, a mhian,
Rinne mé é,
Cé go raibh sé dian agus ródhian,
Chuir mé d'ainm as m'aigne,
Sháigh mé síos é
I gcoirneál cúil na cuimhne.
Chuir mé i dtalamh é
I bhfad ó sholas a haithne ...

Rinne mé mar a dúirt tú, a chroí,
Ach mar shíol,
Phéac d'ainmse sa dorchadas,
Phéac sé agus d'fhás sé
I dtalamh domasaí mo dhoichill
Go dtí gur shín a ghéaga
Aníos agus amach
Fríd bhlaosc mo chinn is mo chéile ....

Dúirt tú liom agus tú ag imeacht
Gan d'ainm a lua níos mó ...

Ach níl leoithne dá dtig
Nach gcluintear an crann seo ag sioscadh ... Joe ... Joe.

You said at the end of our game
Never again to utter your name ...

Yes, my precious, I did as you wished
Truly, I did.
Though hard, much too hard
I flung your name from my mind,
Trampled on it,
In the back corner of my memory
I buried it
Far from the intruding sun.

I did as you asked, beloved,
But like a seed
Your name sprouted in the dark,
Sprouted and grew
In my closed, peaty earth
Until its limbs burst through
And spread
Through my very reason, out through my head.

You said at the end of our game
Never again to utter your name ...

But the slightest breeze that cares to blow
Ruffles that tree, whispers ... Joe ... Joe ...

translated by Gabriel Rosenstock.

In albam na cuimhne atá siad taiscithe
An ceann catach, na súile macánta
agus tráthnónta galánta na Bealtaine.
Samhailteacha! Samhailteacha na cuimhne
as albam i rúnchomhad na haigne
sin a bhfuil iontu, a bhuachaill na Bealtaine,
samhailteacha nach dtéann i ndíchuimhne.

In albam na cuimhne atá siad taiscithe
an ceann catach, na súile macánta
agus tráthnónta galánta na Bealtaine
ach amanta fosclóidh mé rúnchomhad na haigne
agus dhéanfaidh mé iad a aeráil i mo dhánta,
do cheann catach, do shúile macánta
agus tráthnónta galánta na Bealtaine.

SONNET

In memory's album they are stored,
the curly head, the gentle eyes
and those beautiful evenings in May.
Images! Memory's images
from the album of the mind's mysterious keeping.
That's all they are, my *Bealtaine* boy,
images that don't go away.

In memory's album they are stored,
the curly head, the gentle eyes
and a fine May evening
but, times, I will open the mind's secrets
and I will air them in my poems,
your curly head, your gentle eyes
and those beautiful evenings in May.

translated by Gabriel Fitzmaurice

Ní ardaíonn tú i do shuan
Aon tearmann ná daingean

Le linn na hoíche bím ag siúl
I do shaol laistiar de mheall na súl

Atá níos dúchasaí ina ghoirme
Ná sais na Maighdine Muire.

Ar an taobh cúil d'fhocail
Tá a mhacasamhail de shaol.

In your sleep you raise
Neither refuge nor sanctuary

All night I haunt
The hidden world behind your eyes

That is truer blue
Than the Virgin Mary's blouse.

On the hidden side of words
Lies a world of echoed melody.

translated by Joan McBreen.

AOIBH

I spéartha gorma do shúl
ní thiocfaidh cúl ar an lá.

Ní imeoidh cuacha do ghutha
ó dheas uainn mar is gnách.

Ní chaillfidh fuinseoga do ghéag
a gcuid duilleog scáthach.

Ní rachaidh uain óga do gháire
thar aois na bpeataí go brách.

Óir i dTír na nÓg seo do chroí
tá sé ina shíorshamhradh, a ghrá.

BEAUTY

In the blue sky of your eyes,
day will never know demise.

The cuckoos calling from your mouth
will not, as is their wont, fly south.

Ash-branches — your arms and feet
will not lose their sheltered leaves.

The lambs that frisk throughout your laughter
are pet lambkins ever after.

For in your heart's the Land of Youth —
it's summer always there, my Ruth.

translated by Gabriel Fitzmaurice

"Tá stoirm air', adeir tú. 'Stoirm mhillteanach.'
Míshocair, coinníonn tú ag siúl an urláir, síos
agus aníos go truacánta, do shúile impíoch.
Lasmuigh tá an oíche ag séideadh is ag siabadh
timpeall an tí, ag cleataráil ag na fuinneoga,
ag béicíl is ag bagairt trí pholl na heochrach.
'Dhéanfadh sé áit a bhearnú le theacht isteach,'
a deir tú, ag daingniú an dorais le cathaoir uilinne.
Tagann roisteacha fearthainne ag cnagadh
na fuinneoige. De sceit, sciorrann dallóg na cistine
in airde. Creathnaithe, preabann tú as do sheasamh
isteach i m'ucht, ag cuartú dídine.
Ag breith barróige ort, téann mo lámha i ngreim
i do chneas, ag teannadh is ag teannadh. Teas
le teas, scarann do bheola ag súil le póga
díreach is an stoirm ag teacht tríom ina séideoga.
Splancaim is buaileann caor thine do chneas.

154

SHELTER

'It will storm', you said, 'an awful storm'.
Restless, you pace the floor, up
and down plaintively, your eyes suppliant.
Outside the night blows and drifts
about the house, clattering at the windows,
shouting and threatening through the keyhole.
'It would breach a place to come inside',
you say, jamming the door with an armchair.
Volleys of rain knock on the window.
Suddenly, as if in fright, the kitchen blind
rolls up. Quaking, you spring to my breast
for shelter.
Hugging you, my fingers catch
your skin, squeezing, squeezing.
Heat on heat, your lips part to kiss me
as the storm gusts through me.
I flash and a fireball hits your skin.

translated by Gabriel Fitzmaurice

Ar altóir na leapa
ceiliúraim do chorpsa anocht, a ghile,
le deasghnátha mo dhúile.
Gach géag ghrástúil, gach géag mhaighdeanúil
sléachtaim rompu go humhal
is le paidreacha na bpóg
altaím go díograiseach
gach féith is gach féitheog
is cór na gcéadfaí go caithréimeach
ag canadh iomann do do shuáilcí
do bhéal, do bholg, do bhrollach —
tríonóid thintrí an tsóláis.
Is de réir mar a théann
an searmanas i ndéine is i ndlúthpháirtíocht
tá mo bhaill bheatha ar crith
ag fanacht le míorúilt mhacnais
is tiocfaidh, tiocfaidh go fras
nuair a bhlaisfead diamhrachtaí do ghnéis —
cailís an mhiangais
tiocfaidh, áthas na n-áthas
ina shacraimint, ina thabhartas,
ina theangacha tine an eolais.
Tiocfaidh
réamhaisnéis na bhflaitheas.

On the altar of the bed
I celebrate your body tonight, my love,
with the rites of my desire.
I humbly kneel before
each graceful limb, each virgin limb
and with kisses of prayer
I fervently give thanks
for every sinew, every muscle
while triumphantly the senses' choir
is singing hymns to your pleasure
your mouth, your belly, your breast —
the fiery trinity of joy.
And as the ceremony intensifies
in solidarity
my body trembles
expecting the miracle
which will come voluptuously
when I taste the mystery of your sex —
the chalice of desire.
It will come, joy of joys,
a sacrament, a gift,
the fiery tongues of knowledge
and I will have
intimations of heaven.

translated by Gabriel Fitzmaurice

Cneas le cneas, a chroí
dhéanfaidh salann ár gcuid allais
sáile den leabaidh

Béal ar bhéal go docht
beidh bradán feasa do theanga
ag snámh ionam anocht.

KNOWLEDGE

Skin pressed to skin, my heart,
Salt of our sweat
Churning the sheets to a sea.

Mouth pressed firmly to mouth,
The salmon of knowledge — your tongue —
Tonight will swim in me.

translated by Gabriel Rosenstock

Snaidhmeann tú do ghéaga thart orm anocht
is gaoth ár gcéadfaí ár séideadh le chéile;
crann silíní mise géilliúil i ngúna bándearg
agus is tusa crann darach fearúil is lán d'fhéile.

Is tusa an crann darach a thugann dídean
don taistealaí a thuirsíonn ionam i lár na hoíche;
Is tusa an crann darach a thugann dearcáin
don pháiste a shúgraíonn asam oíche na gaoithe.

Muidinne na crainn atá scartha óna chéile ar an tsliabh.
Ní fhaca tú ár ngéaga ag dlúthú le chéile ariamh.
Ár gcinniúint adeir tú bheith deighilte ó luan go luan.
Amaidí! Tá ár gcuid rútaí ag muirniú a chéile go buan.

TREES

You knot your limbs around me tonight,
the wind of our senses blows us together;
a cherry tree, I surrender in my pink dress;
you are an oak, manly and generous.

You are the oak that shelters
the traveller who tires in me at midnight;
you are the oak that gives an acorn
to the child who plays out of me on a windy night.

We are separate trees on a hill,
you haven't seen our boughs meet still.
It's fate that parts us loin from loin.
Nonsense! Our roots caress till the end of time.

translated by Gabriel Fitzmaurice

Tá soilse bithbhuan' na spéire
Ag spréacharnaigh anocht go glé
Gach ceann acu ina mheall mistéire
Ach ní orthu atá m'iúl, a bhé,

Ach ar chruinneog chré do chinn
As a dtigeann drithlí órbhuí na gcúl;
Soilse spéiriúla i ngach aird go glinn —
Gile an gháire agus gorm tintrí na súl.

Ach do cheann meallach bheith ar m'ucht,
Dhearmadfainn díomuaine an Duine,
Ó i bhfirmimint d'fhoiltse anocht,
Thrasnóinn Bealach na Bó Finne.

The everlasting firmament
Is sparkling bright tonight,
Each star an orb of mystery,
But, love, I pay no thought,

To any but the sparkling world
Golden in your hair —
Bright laughter, blue flashing eyes
Vivid everywhere.

To have your head entice my breast,
I'd forget life's day-to-day:
In the firmament of your hair
I'd cross the Milky Way.

translated by Gabriel Fitzmaurice

B'fhearr liomsa buachaill thí an leanna
a bhfuil a chroí lán de theas ceana

Is a labhrann i laomanna lasánta
faoina dhuáilcí is faoina dhánta

Is a dhéanann gáire chomh gríosaitheach
le craos de mhóin chípíneach

Is a chaitheann spréachta óna shúile
a lasann tinidh mo dhúile

Ná Nefertítí í féin i mo leabaidh
is iontaisí na bhFaróanna ar fud an tí.

You bar boy, you — yes, any time,
Your glowing heart is mine.

When you speak flames flicker and glow,
passionate poetry in your eyes of sloe.

Your laughter smoulders, is bright surf
is blue flame from dry turf.

You ignite me with your gaze,
lust encompasses all my days.

Take me, take me to your bed.
Who needs Nefertiti? She's dead!

translated by Gabriel Rosenstock.

Anocht agus tú sínte síos le mo thaobh
a chaoin mhic an cheana, do chorp
teann téagartha, aoibh na hóige ort,
      anseo tá mé sábháilte
cuachta go docht faoi scáth d'uchta:
sleánna cosanta do sciathán
      mo chrioslú go dlúth
óir is tusa mo laoch, an curadh caol cruaidh
a sheasann idir mé agus uaigneas tíoránta na hoíche.

Is tusa mo laoch, mo thréan is mo neart,
mo Chú na gCleas agus níl fhios agam i gceart
cé acu an luan laoich é seo
      atá ag teacht ó do chneas
nó gríos gréine. Ach is cuma. Tá mé buíoch as an teas,
as na dealraitheacha deasa ó do ghrua
      a ghealaíonn mo dhorchadas,
as an dóigh a ndéanann tú an t-uaigneas
a dhiongbháil domh le fíochmhaireacht do ghrá.

Anocht má tá cath le fearadh agat, a ghrá,
bíodh sé anseo i measc na bpiliúr:
Craith do sciath agus gread do shleá,
      beartaigh do chlaíomh
go beacht. Lig gáir churaidh as do bhráid.
Luífidh mé anseo ag baint sásamh súl
      as a bhfuil den fhear
ag bogadaí ionat, a dhúil, go ndéanfaidh tú do bhealach féin
a bhearnú chugam fríd plúid agus piliúr.

Now, tonight, streched by my side
delightful lad, your strong
sinewy limbs smile youthfully,
            here I'm safe a while
squirrelling up to your trunk:
your limbs are swift spears
            fending off the world
my champion, proud sleek warrior
you man the gap between me and night's tyranny.

My solace, my defence, my fortress,
Playful Hound, how can I tell
is it the valour-halo
            which emanates from your skin
or sun-glow? No matter, I'm grateful for the warmth,
those darting rays from your cheek
            that illuminate the obscurity;
how you match my wretchedness
with the savagery of your love.

Tonight, sweet soul, should you declare battle
let it be here among pillows:
let your shield shudder, aim your spear,
            let your sword be ready
and true. Shout aloud your war-cry.
Here I'll lie, my eyes entranced
            as your manliness
moves and — darling — I lie in the breach,
in the theatre of linen.

Agus is toil liom, a mhacaoimh óig
gurb anseo ar léana mo leapa
a dhéanfá le barr feabhais
            do mhacghníomhartha macnais,
gurb anseo i ngleannta is i gcluanta
mo cholla, a thiocfá i dteann is i dtreise
            is go mbeadh gach ball
do mo bhallaibh, ag síorthabhairt grá duit
ar feadh síoraíocht na hoíche seo.

Anocht chead ag an domhan ciorclú
leis na beo is leis na mairbh:
Anseo i dtearmann dlúth na bpóg
            tá an saol ina stad:
Anseo i ndún daingean do bhaclainne
tá cúl ar chlaochlú. I bhfad uainn
            mairgí móra an tsaoil:
na tíortha is na treabha a dhéanfadh cocstí
de cheithre creasa na cruinne lena gcuid cogaíochta.

Anocht, a mhacaoimh óig, bainimis fad saoil
as gach cogar, gach caoinamharc, gach cuimilt.
Amárach beidh muid gafa mar is gnáth
            i gcasadh cinniúnach na beatha,
i gcealg is i gcluain na Cinniúna.
Amárach díolfar fiacha na fola is na feola
            ach anocht, a fhir óig álainn,
tá muid i gciorcal draíochta an ghrá.
Ní bhuafaidh codladh orainn ná crá.

And how I desire, nimble Hound,
that here on this white plain
you should surpass yourself
              in thrust and swagger:
here in the recesses and glens
of my body come with your assault
              so that every rock and fern
cries out in sweetest anguish
the long night through.

Let the world on its axis turn
with all the living and the dead;
here in the sanctuary of lips
              our world ends.
Here in the citadel of your arms
time has run out. The world's misery
              an aeon away,
nations and tribes, fighting it out,
              all day, every day.

Tonight, Hound of Ulster, let each whisper,
each glance, each touch be for ever.
Tomorrow we shall be, again, like all others,
              fulfilling our fateful rounds —
the deceit and treachery of it all!
Tomorrow the debt of flesh and blood must be paid,
              but tonight, my lone warrior,
the chalice is moist at the brim
And — miserable sleep! — stay away from him.

                    translated by Gabriel Rosenstock.

Tá sé seachantach
Seachantach agus doicheallach
Mo sheanchara a bhí chomh aigeanta
A bhí chomh saor ó chrá croí
Le scológ cheoil an smólaigh.
Anois tá sé tostach
Tostach agus diúltach
Agus é ag conlú chuige féin go dúranta
Ag cúngú le méid a léin
Isteach i bpríosún dá dhéanamh féin
Agus ó chuir sé a aigne faoi ghlas
An doichill, d'imigh sé as aithne
Óir cha scéitheann sé a smaointe
Le héinne, fiú go briste i dtocht chaointe
Agus braithim an buaireamh ag borradh
Ina chliabh, ag cruinniú agus ag creimeadh
Agus is eagla liom pléascadh
Ach ní pléascadh a thig
Ach Osna
Agus is cosúil an Osna
Le siosarnach gaoithe
I dtithe tréigthe Mhín na Craoibhe,
Le glug glag an Gheimhridh
I bpoill bháite na Míne Buí.

Bhí mise go muiníneach tráth
Is mo chroí níor cheil mé ar chách
Ach rinne cailleach dímheasúil na cinniúna
Ceap magaidh de mo ghrá;
Is anois tá mé seachantach
Anois tá mé doicheallach
Is braithim in amanta i bpubanna

170

He is distant,
distant and churlish,
my old friend who was cheerful
as the thrush's songburst.
Now he is silent,
    silent and negative
shrinking into himself sullenly
narrowing into a prison
of his own making.
And since he locked up his mind
unwelcomingly, he's beyond recognition
refusing to share his thoughts
with any
even breaking down in a fit of crying
and I feel frustration swelling
in his side, gathering and gnawing
and I fear he'll explode
    but no!
    Nothing but a Sigh,
a Sigh like
    the wind's whispering
    through abandoned houses in Mín na Craoibhe,
    plop-plop of Winter
    in the marsh-holes of Mín Buí.

I was full of confidence once
and didn't conceal my heart from anyone
but the contemptuous hag of Fate
mocked my love
    and now I'm distant,
    now I'm churlish
and, at times, I feel in crowded

171

Pluchtachta, pleascadh ag corraí i mo chroí
Ach ní pléascadh a thig
    Ach Osna
Agus is cosúil an Osna
    Le siosarnach gaoithe
    I dtithe tréigthe Mhín na Craoibhe;
    Le glug glag an gheimhridh
    I bpoill bháite na Míne Buí.

A sheanchara sheachantaigh,
A sheanchara dhoicheallaigh,
Suímís síos mar ba ghnáth
Is líonaimis gloine dá chéile
Thart ar thinidh na féile
Is ligimis Osna,
    An t-am seo le chéile.

pubs an explosion building up in my heart
  but no explosion comes
  but a Sigh,
a Sigh like
  the wind's whispering
  through abandoned houses in Mín na Craoibhe,
  plop-plop of Winter
  in the marsh-holes of Mín Buí.

My old, distant friend,
my old, churlish friend
let's sit down as we used to
and drink each others' health
around a hospitable fire
and let's sigh
  This time together.

translated by Gabriel Fitzmaurice

Caoineadh na gcrotach i bhfásach na hoíche,
tá siad mar chroíthe cráite.

Níl ann ach go gcoinníonn néalta cúl ar dheora.
Éalaíonn osna ón spéir.

Cneadaíonn an ghealach codladh na locha
lena cumraíocht dofhaighte;

Díreach mar a chneadaíonn tusa gach oíche
duibheagáin dhubha m'aigne,

le do scáthchruth glé dofhulaingthe
nach ruaigfear go réidh.

Anois tá muid deighilte ó chéile go brách
amhail línte comhthreomhara,

Is muid ag gabháil taobh le taobh, a shaobhghrá,
tostach gan teagmháil.

Ach anuraidh, anseo ag ceann Loch an Ghainimh,
oíche is an spéir ag spraoi,

Thrasnaigh muid ár gcoirp is ár gcinniúint faoi thrí
i sceitimíní an ghrá,

Is bhí ár leabaidh luachra lán de shabhaircíní
is de shamhailtí greannmhara;

Ach níl sna sabhaircíní anocht ach fiailí
seachas "smugaí na sióg",

174

Cries of the curlews in waste places of the night,
they are like broken hearts.

All that's happening is that clouds turn their back on tears.
Sighs escape from the sky.

The moon comes ravelling the sleep of the lake
with its unattainable dreams;

In the same way that you, each night, come ravelling
the black depths of my mind

With your unbearable bright shadowshape
that won't be easily banished.

Now we are parted from one another forever
as parallel lines are parted,

And we are travelling, my heart's love, side by side
in silence, without touching.

Still, last year, here at the head of Loch an Ghainimh
at night, while the sky was playful

Three times we crossed our bodies and our destinies
in the ecstasies of love;

Our bed of rushes then was alive with primroses
and with sunfilled images;

But tonight the primroses are only weeds
rather than the "fairies' snots",

Is ní "spagetti na gcaorach" iad a thuilleadh
na tomóga beaga luachra.

Caoineadh na gcrotach i bhfásach na hoíche
Tá siad mar chroíthe cráite,

Is ón chrá d'fhág tú i mo chroíse, dubhaigh, a scáth!
isteach in uaigh na díchuimhne!

Nor are they the "sheeps' spaghetti" either,
the little clumps of rushes.

Cries of the curlews in waste places of the night,
they are like broken hearts,

And out of the torment you left in my heart, depart,
o shadow, into the grave of oblivion.

translated by John F. Deane

Do Richard agus Sandra

Cérbh as í murarbh ón tsáile í? Caidé
eile a réiteodh
le feamainn rua na ndual, le glas na súl,
le suathadh síoraí
an bhrollaigh, le cáitheadh cúrach
na hanála adaí.

Is mar thiontódh trá i Machaire Rabhartaigh
chas sí uaim i dtobainne
is ina diaidh níl fágtha ach raic na gcuimhní
ar chladaí m'intinne;
carraig chreimthe an chroí agus och,
na deora goirte.

SEA-WOMAN

For Richard and Sandra

Where was she from if not the sea? What
else explains
that seaweed-auburn hair, those grey-green eyes,
the ceaseless agitation
of her breast, the foaming spume
of her breath.

And as the tide turns in Machaire Rabhartaigh
she turned from me suddenly
leaving only the wrack of memories
on the shore of my mind;
the abraded rock of the heart, and O,
the salt tears.

translated by Aodán Mac Póilín

Tá mé ag tarraingt ar bharr na Bealtaine
go dúchroíoch i ndorchacht na hoíche
ag ardú malacha i m'aistear is i m'aigne
ag cur in aghaidh bristeacha borba gaoithe.

B'ise mo mhaoinín, b'ise mo Ghort a'Choirce
mise a thug a cuid fiántais chun míntíreachais
ach tá a claonta dúchais ag teacht ar ais arís
anocht bhí súile buí i ngort na seirce.

Tím Véineas ansiúd os cionn Dhún Lúiche
ag caochadh anuas lena súile striapaí
agus ar ucht na Mucaise siúd cíoch na gealaí
ag gobadh as gúna dubh na hoíche.

Idir dólás agus dóchas, dhá thine Bhealtaine,
caolaím d'aon rúid bhuile mar leathdhuine.
Tá soilse an ghleanna ag crith os mo choinne —
faoi mhalaí na gcnoc sin iad súile Shuibhne.

I am making for the summit of Bealtaine
My heart heavy in the black of night
Scaling the rockface of mind and matter
Defending myself in the wind's harsh fight.

She was my wealth, she my harvest.
Her wild country made fertile by my hand
But the natural barrenness creeps back once more
Tonight there were weeds choking the land.

I see Venus over Dún Lúiche
Staring down with her *whoring* eyes
And the streak of the moon in Mucaise's lap
Rents the black dress of night's disguise.

Between horror and hope, two flames of Bealtaine,
I swing in one movement as madmen will
The lights in the valley tremble before me
And Sweeney's eyes are below the hill.

translated by Sarah Berkeley

Do Sheán Ó Brollaigh

Mura mothaíonn tú
beat buile an dáin
Le d'intleacht
ná cáin d'éirim cinn, a Sheáin:
Tá gach ní i gceart ach amháin
an modh scrúdaithe.

Ach le do mhéarasa, fiach
go díreach
mar a dhéanfadh dochtúir
frithbhualadh na bhfocal
is láithreach
ó luas taomach a gcuislí
mothóidh tú
tinneas croí mo dháin.

SONNET

For Seán Ó Brollaigh

If you don't feel
the mad pulse of the poem
with your intellect
don't condemn your intelligence, Seán:
Everything's O.K. but
the manner of your examination.

but with your finger, seek,
exactly as a doctor,
the throbbing of the words
and immediately
from the erratic pulse-beat
you will feel
the sickness in the heart of my poem.

translated by Gabriel Fitzmaurice

TRANSUBSTAINTIÚ

Do Vona Lynn

Idir an smaoineamh agus an briathar
tá dúichí oighir agus ceo.

Ach beidh mise le mo bheo
ag cascairt an tseaca, ag scaipeadh an cheo

ag gríosú is ag grianadh
le gaetha tintrí mo chroí

ionas go dtiocfaidh tú fós i mbláth,
tusa nach bhfuil ionat ach scáil.

TRANSUBSTANTIATION

For Vona Lynn

Between the thought and the word
are regions of ice and fog;

but all my life I'll be
shattering the frost, scattering the fog

stirring and sunning
with my heart's fiery rays

so that you'll flower one day
you that are only a shadow.

translated by Gabriel Fitzmaurice

do Mháirtín Ó Direáin

Is tusa an fuascailteoir
a ghríosaigh is a threoraigh le do theacht
éirí amach na bhfocal.

As daingne díchuimhne
shaoraigh tú iad ó dhaorsmacht
le heochair d'inchinne.

Saoránaigh iad anois
a bhfuil a gcearta acu go beacht
i bpoblacht do dháin.

THE LIBERATOR

for Máirtín Ó Direáin

You are the Emancipator,
Who fired and steered with your coming
The Rising of the Words.

From the fortress of amnesia,
You loosed them from bondage,
With your cerebral key.

Now they are free,
Who have their charter enshrined
In the Republic of your song.

translated by Frank Galligan.

DO JACK KEROUAC

do Shéamas de Bláca

> *"The only people for me are the mad ones,*
> *the ones who are mad to live, mad to talk,*
> *mad to be saved, desirous of everything at*
> *the same time, the ones who never yawn or*
> *say a commonplace thing but burn,*
> *burn like fabulous yellow roman candles"*
>
> Sliocht as *On the Road*

Ag sioscadh trí do shaothar anocht tháinig leoithne na
cuimhne chugam ó gach leathanach.

Athmhúsclaíodh m'óige is mhothaigh mé ag éirí ionam an
beat brionglóideach a bhí ag déanamh aithris ort i dtús na seachtóidí.

1973. Bhí mé *hookáilte* ort. Lá i ndiaidh lae fuair mé *shot* inspioráide ó do
shaothar a ghealaigh m'aigne is a shín mo shamhlaíocht.

Ní Mín 'a Leá ná Fána Bhuí a bhí á fheiceáil agam an t-am adaí ach
machairí Nebraska agus táilte féaraigh Iowa.

Agus nuair a thagadh na *bliúanna* orm ní bealach na Bealtaine a bhí
romham amach ach mórbhealach de chuid Mheiriceá.

"Hey man you gotta stay high" a déarfainn le mo chara agus muid ag
freakáil trí Chailifornia Chill Ulta isteach go Frisco an Fhál Charraigh.

Tá do leabhar ina luí druidte ar m'ucht ach faoi chraiceann an chlúdaigh
tá do chroí ag preabadaigh i bhféitheog gach focail.

Oh man mothaím arís, na *higheanna* adaí ar Himiléithe na hóige:

Ó chósta go cósta thriall muid le chéile, saonta, spleodrach, místiúrtha;

Oilithreacht ordóige ó Nua-Eabhrac go Frisco agus as sin go Cathair
Mheicsiceo;

Beat buile inár mbeatha. Spreagtha. Ag bladhmadh síos bóithre i
gCadillacs ghasta ag sciorradh thar íor na céille ar eiteoga na m*bennies.*

Thrasnaigh muid teorainneacha agus thrasnaigh muid taibhrithe.

Cheiliúraigh muid gach casadh ar bhealach ár mbeatha, *binge*anna agus

188

TO JACK KEROUAC

For Séamas de Bláca

> *"The only people for me are the mad ones,*
> *the ones who are mad to live, mad to talk,*
> *mad to be saved, desirous of everything at*
> *the same time, the ones who never yawn or*
> *say a commonplace thing but burn, burn like*
> *fabulous yellow roman candles"*

On the Road

Thumbing through your work tonight the aroma of memories came from
    every page.
My youth rewoke and I felt rising in me the dreamy beat that imitated
    you at the start of the '70s.
1973. I was hooked on you. Day after day I got shots of inspirration from
    your life which lit my mind and stretched my imagination.
I didn't see Mín 'a Leá or Fána Bhuí then, but the plains of Nebraska and
    the grassy lands of Iowa
And when the blues came it wasn't the Bealtaine road that beckoned but
    a way stretching across America.
"Hey man you gotta stay high," I'd say to my friend as we freaked
    through California's Cill Ulta into Frisco's Falcarragh.

Your book lies shut on my breast, your heart beating under the skin cover
    in the muscle of every word.
Oh man I feel them again, those highs on youth's Himalayas from coast
    to coast we roamed together, free, wild, reckless:
A hitchhiking odyssey from New York to Frisco and down to Mexico
    City.
A mad beat to our lives. Crazed. Hurtling down highways in speeding
    cars, skidding over the verge of sanity on the wings of Benzedrine.
We crossed frontiers and we scaled dreams.
Celebrations at every turn of life's highway, binges and brotherhood

bráithreachas ó Bhrooklyn go Berkeley, *booze, bop* agus Búdachas; Éigse na
hÁise; sreangscéalta as an tsíoraíocht ar na Sierras; marijuana agus
misteachas i Meicsiceo; brionglóidí buile i mBixby Canyon.

Rinne muid Oirféas as gach *orifice.*

Ó is cuimhneach liom é go léir, a Jack, an chaint is an cuartú.
Ba tusa bard beoshúileach na mbóithre, ar thóir na foirfeachta, ar thóir na
bhFlaitheas.
Is cé nach bhfuil aon aicearra chuig na Déithe, adeirtear, d'éirigh leatsa slí
a aimsiú in amantaí nuair a d'fheistigh tú úim adhainte ar Niagara
d'aigne le *dope* is le diagacht.
Is i mBomaite sin na Buile gineadh solas a thug spléachadh duit ar an
tSíoraíocht,
Is a threoraigh 'na bhaile tú, tá súil agam, lá do bháis chuig Whitman,
Proust agus Rimbaud.

Tá mo bhealach féin romham amach… *"a road that ah zigzags all over
creation. Yeah man! Ain't nowhere else it can go. Right!"*
Agus lá inteacht ar bhealach na seanaoise is na scoilteacha
Nó lá níos cóngaraí do bhaile, b'fhéidir,
Scroicfidh mé Crosbhealach na Cinniúna is beidh an Bás romham ansin,
Treoraí tíriúil le mé a thabhairt thar teorainn,
Is ansin, *goddammit* a Jack, beidh muid beirt ag síobshiúl sa tSíoraíocht.

from Brooklyn to Berkeley; booze, bop and Buddhism; Asian verse;
    telegrams from a Sierra eternity; marijuana and mysticism in
    Mexico; frenzied visions in Bixby Canyon.

Orpheus emerged from every orifice.

O I remember it all Jack, the talk and the quest.
You were the wild-eyed poet walking free, searching for harmony,
    searching for Heaven.
And although it is said there's no shortcut to the Gods you opened one
    up now and then, harnessing your mind's Niagara with dope and
    divinity.
And in those rapturous moments you generated the
    light that you saw eternity by
And that guided you, I hope, the day of your death, home to Whitman,
    Proust and Rimbaud.

My road is before me "a road that ah zigzags all over creation. Yeah man!
    Ain't nowhere else it can go. Right!"
And someday, on the road of failing sight and knotted limbs
Or a less distant day, perhaps
Death will face me at Fate's Crossroads
My gentle companion across the frontier
And then, goddamit Jack, we'll both be hiking across eternity.

                                        translated by Sarah Berkeley

AN CROÍ BA SHÚ TALÚN

"Tá sú an tsamhraidh
ag borradh i ngach beo,"
a dúirt sé go haiféalach
agus muid ag féachaint amach
trí fhuinneog an tseomra suí
ar theaghlaigh óga na sráide
ag súgradh ar an fhaiche.

"Ach ó dódh Bríd is na páistí
tarraingíodh mo chuid rútaí
glan amach as an talamh,"
is ní raibh ann ní ba mhó
ach cnámharlach folamh
ag críonadh is ag seargadh
ar charn fuílligh na beatha.

Thiontaigh sé chugam,
lí an bháis ina dhreach
is ó chaileandar beag dialainne
a bhí caite ar bhord agam
stróic sé na leathnaigh, mí ar mhí,
á rá nach raibh i ndán dó feasta
ach dorchadas agus díomua.

Ar a imeacht uaim, seachas slán
a fhágáil agam, phioc sé cnapán
beag dearg as mias na dtorthaí
agus bhronn orm é go tostach —
sú talún a bhí ann, lán
de shúmhaireacht dhearg an tsamhraidh —
an oíche sin théacht a chroí.

STRAWBERRY HEART

"The sap of the summer
Is pulsing in everyone,"
He said with sorrow,
As we gazed
Through the sitting-room window
at the street children
Playing on the lawn.

"But since the burning of Bríd and the wanes,
My roots have been torn
Clean out of the ground."
And there was nothing to him
But an empty shell,
Growing and decaying
On the leavings of life.

He turned to me,
Death's pallor in his eyes,
And from a little monthly diary
I had left down on the table,
He tore the pages, one by one,
And said for him there was only
The darkness and despair along the way.

On his way out, besides him saying
Farewell, he picked a small red
drop from the bowl of fruit
And silently presented it to me.
It was a strawberry — bursting
With the red succulence of summer —
That night his heart stopped.

Nuair a fheicim sú talún anois
ní meas méith a shamhlaím leis
ach uafás, uafás agus samhnas.
Cnapán créachta fola
a thaibhsíonn chugam, a Mhuiris,
bliain tar éis imeacht na himeachta —
croí téachta, croí téachta.

When I see a strawberry now
It's not a sweet fruit I perceive
But horror and the taste of terror.
A clot of blood is what I see
Before my eyes, Muiris,
A year since your demise,
your damaged heart, your damaged heart.

translated by Frank Galligan.

Do Des Lynn

I dtráth agus in antráth
coinníonn sé súil ghéar ar ghairdín na n-úll.

Díbríonn sé a chlann ar shiúl
Ádhamh agus Éabha de bharr alpadh na n-úll.

Tá a chroí is cosúil
i bpióga úll. Tinneas an tsaoil nó saobhdhúil?

Tá sé doiligh a rá
mar nach gceadóidh sé scrúdú dochtúra

ná ceistiú go brách.

For Des Lynn

From early hours to late
he keeps a sharp eye on Eden's gate.

He evicts his own Family,
Adam and Eve, because of what they ate.

His heart, it would appear,
Is lost to apple-tarts. Is he world-weary or somewhat queer?

Difficult to relate
since he refuses to be psycho-analysed

or scrutinized.

translated by Gabriel Rosenstock

Ní chasfaidh tusa thart do chloigeann
agus an bás ag rolladh chugat mar an t-aigéan.

Coinneoidh tú ag stánadh air go seasta
agus é ag scuabadh chugat isteach ina spraisteacha geala
ó fhíor na síoraíochta.
Coinneoidh tú do chiall
agus do chéadfaí agus é ag siollfarnaigh
thar chladaí d'inchinne
go dtí go mbeidh sé ar d'aithne
go huile agus go hiomlán
díreach mar a rinne tú agus tú i do thachrán
ar thránna Mhachaire Rabhartaigh
agus tonnta mara an Atlantaigh
ag sealbhú do cholainne.
Ach sula ndeachaigh do shaol ar neamhní
shroich tusa ciumhais an chladaigh.
Tarlóidh a mhacasamhail anseo.
Sroichfidh tú domhan na mbeo
tar éis dul i dtaithí an duibheagáin le d'aigne;
ach beidh séala an tsáile ort go deo,
beidh doimhneacht agat mar dhuine:
as baol an bháis tiocfaidh fírinne.

Ní thabharfainn de shamhail duit i mo dhán
ach iadsan i gcoillte Cholumbia
ar léigh mé fá dtaobh daofa sa leabharlann:
dream a chaitheann píopaí daite créafóige, píopaí
nár úsáideadh riamh lena ndéanamh
ach scaobóga créafóige
a baineadh i mbaol beatha

THE CLAY PIPES

You won't be the one to turn away when death
rolls in towards you like the ocean.

You will hold to your steadfast gaze,
as it comes tiding in, all plash and glitter
from the rim of eternity.
You will keep your head.
You will come to your senses again as it
foams over the ridged beaches of your brain
and you will take it all in
and know it completely:
you will be a child again, out on the strand
at Magheraroarty, your body
abandoned altogether
to the lift of the Atlantic.
But before you went the whole way then away
into nothingness, you would touch the bottom.
And this will be what happens to you here:
You'll go through a black hole of initiation,
then reach the land of the living;
but the seal of the brine will be on you forever
and you'll have depth as a person:
You'll walk from danger of death into the truth.

Here is the best image I can find:
you are like the forest people of Columbia
I read about in the library,
a tribe who smoke clay pipes, coloured pipes
that used to have to be made from this one thing:
basketfuls of clay
scooped out in fatal danger

i ndúichí sean-namhad, gleann scáthach
timepallaithe le gaistí, gardaí agus saigheada nimhe.
Dar leo siúd a deir an t-alt tuairisce
nach bhfuil píopaí ar bith iomlán,
seachas na cinn a bhfuil baol
ag baint le soláthar a gcuid créafóige.

in enemy country, in a scaresome place
full of traps and guards and poisoned arrows.
According to this article, they believe
that the only fully perfect pipes
are ones made out of the clay
collected under such extreme conditions.

translated by Seamus Heaney

Do Jarleth Donnelly

Mise Charlie an scibhí,
lán eadóchais agus crá
ag caidreamh liom féin
ar mo lá *off* ón Óstán;
síos agus aníos Hyde Park
ar fán i measc scuainí
doicheallach an Domhnaigh
is a Raiftearaí, *fuck this for a lark.*

Ach ina dhiaidh sin agus uile
sáraíonn orthu mé a chloí
agus amanta i splanc díchéillí
lasann mo chroí le díogras
diabhalta domhínithe na hóige
agus títhear domh go bhfuil oifigí
urghránna na gcomhlachtaí gnó
chomh caoin le húrchnoic mo chuimhne.

Ach bíonn amanta ann fosta —
laethanta bó riabhaí na haigne
agus ní bhíonn ann ach go mbím
ábalta mo cheann a ardú
agus mo shúile a dhíriú
ar na hUafaisí. Tráthnónta geimhridh
agus an dorchadas ag teacht anuas orm
i gcruthaíocht *vacuum cleaner,*

'mo shú isteach go craosach
i bpoll guairneáin lagmhisnigh;
Agus sa tslí sin agus a leithéidí

202

I AM CHARLIE THE SKIVVY

For Jarleth Donnelly

I am Charlie the skivvy
Full of anguish and despair
Keeping myself company
On my day off from the Hotel;
Up and down Hyde Park
Wandering among the hostile
Sunday queues
And Raftery, fuck this for a lark.

But nevertheless
They fail to break me
And sometimes with a foolish spark
My heart lights with the mischievous
Inexplicable enthusiasm of youth
And the hideous company offices
Seem to me as gentle
As the refreshing hills of my youth.

But there are other times —
The Borrowing Days of the mind
When I can hardly lift my head
And direct my eyes at
The Horrors. Winter evenings
Especially, with the darkness
Descending upon me
Like a vacuum cleaner,

Sucking me greedily into
Its vortex of disheartenment
And in such ways

téann snáithe mo shaoil
agus mo scéil in aimhréidh
i gcathair ghríobháin an tseachráin
agus ní bhíonn mo theangaidh
i ndán mé a thabhairt slán

ón Bhaol. Teangaidh bhocht an tsléibhe!
I gculaith ghlas caorach
an tseansaoil, tá sí chomh saonta
liom féin, i *slickness* na cathrach;
chomh hamscaí faoi na soilse seo
le damhsóir bróga tairní
i *mballet* Rúiseach. Ach lá inteacht
tiocfaidh muid beirt, b'fhéidir,

Ar phéirspicíocht dár gcuid féin
a bhéarfas muinín dúinn
ár n-aghaidh a thabhairt go meanmnach
ar ár ndán; tráth a mbeidh
ár mbriathra ag teacht go hiomlán
lenár mbearta, is cuma cé chomh fada
agus a bheas muid ar fán
ónár ndomhan dúchais.

Féach anois mé is mo chúl
le balla i dTrafalgar Square,
ag dúil le bogstócach ón bhaile
atá amuigh ag déanamh aeir
mo dhálta féin, agus mura raibh
a dhath níos aeraí á bhíogadh,
sure, thig linn suí anseo, taobh
le taobh agus glúin le glúin, go ciúin,

ag éisteacht le colúir ár gcuimhní
ag cuachaireacht i gcomhthiúin.

My life's thread becomes entangled
In the confusing maze of the city
And my tongue cannot rescue me

From the Danger, the poor old mountain Tongue!
Clad in old world homespun
She is as gullible as myself
In the city slickness;
As ungainly under these lights
As a hobnailed stepdancer
In a Russian ballet. But some day
Perhaps we will both discover

A perspective of our own
Which will give us confidence
To face our destiny with courage;
When our words will completely
Match our deeds, no matter
How far we stray
From our native world.

Look at me now, my back
To a wall in Trafalgar Square
Expecting a youngster from home
Who is out taking the air
Just like me, and if there is nothing
More exciting stirring in him
Sure, we can sit here, side by side,
Knees touching, quietly,

And listen to the doves of our memories
Cooing harmoniously.

translated by Lillis Ó Laoire

Do Liam Desmond

Mar bhláth fosclaíonn an ghrian amach
os cionn na cathrach —
Tiúilip teicnidhaite an tSamhraidh —
Agus cé gur minic a chaill mé mo mhuinín
agus m'aisling anseo i mbéal na séibe
agus cé go mbím goiríneach
ó am go ham le *acne* na haigne
inniu aoibhním agus tig luisne
na mochmhaidine amach ar mo dhreach.

Anois piocaim suas Mín 'a Leá agus Mayfair
ar an mhinicíocht
mhire mhíorúilteacht amháin i m'aigne
sa *bhuzz* seo a mhothaím i mBerkley Square;
agus mé ag teacht orm féin le dearfacht
nár mhothaigh mé go dtí seo
mo *vibe* féin, mo rithim féin,
rithim bheo na beatha ag borradh agus ag *buzzáil*
i bhféitheacha mo bhriathra.

Mar thréad caorach á gcur chun an tsléibhe
tá'n trácht ag méileach
go míshuimhneach ar na bóithre seo
ó Phark Lane go Piccadilly
agus sna ceithre hairde
tá na hoifigí... séibhte glasliatha na cathrach
á ngrianú agus á n-aoibhniú féin
faoi sholas na Bealtaine:
Don chéad uair braithim sa bhaile i gcéin.

For Liam Desmond

Like a flower the sun opens out
Above the city —
Technicoloured summer tulip —
And although I have often suddenly lost my courage
And my vision here
Although my mind is sometimes
Pimply with acne
Today I rejoice and the early morning
Glow pervades my appearance.

Now I pick up Mín 'a Leá and Mayfair
On the same mad miraculous
Frequency in my mind
In this buzz I feel in Berkeley Square;
While I discover myself with a positiveness
I haven't already felt
My own vibe, my own rhythm
The exciting rhythm of life increasing and buzzing
In the arteries that are my words.

Like a flock of sheep being driven to the mountain
The traffic is bleating
Uneasily on the roads
From Park Lane to Piccadilly
And in all directions
The offices... grey green city mountains
Sun themselves and rejoice in the May sunshine:
For the first time I feel at home abroad.

translated by Lillis Ó Laoire

CAOINEADH

(I gcuimhne mo mháthar)

Chaoin mé na cuileatacha ar ucht mo mháthara
An lá a bhásaigh Mollie — peata de sheanchaora
Istigh i gcreagacha crochta na Beithí.
Á cuartú a bhí muid lá marbhánta samhraidh
Is brú anála orainn beirt ag dreasú na gcaorach
Siar ó na hailltreacha nuair a tímid an marfach
Sna beanna dodhreaptha. Préacháin dhubha ina scaotha
Á hithe ina beatha gur imigh an dé deiridh aisti
De chnead choscrach amháin is gan ionainn iarraidh
Tharrthála a thabhairt uirthi thíos sna scealpacha.
Ní thiocfaí mé a shásamh is an tocht ag teacht tríom;
D'fháisc lena hucht mé is í ag cásamh mo chaill liom
Go dtí gur chuireas an racht adaí ó íochtar mo chroí.
D'iompair abhaile mé ansin ar a guailneacha
Ag gealladh go ndéanfadh sí ceapairí arán préataí.

Inniu tá mo Theangaidh ag saothrú an bháis.
Ansacht na bhfilí—teangaidh ár n-aithreacha
Gafa i gcreagacha crochta na Faillí
Is gan ionainn í a tharrtháil le dásacht.
Cluinim na smeachannaí deireanacha
Is na héanacha creiche ag teacht go tapaidh,
A ngoba craosacha réidh chun feille.
Ó dá ligfeadh sí liú amháin gaile — liú catha
A chuirfeadh na creachadóirí chun reatha,
Ach seo í ag creathnú, seo í ag géilleadh;
Níl mo mháthair anseo le mé a shuaimhniú a thuilleadh
Is ní dhéanfaidh gealladh an phian a mhaolú.

LAMENT

(In memory of my mother)

I cried on my mother's breast, cried sore
The day Mollie died, our old pet ewe
Trapped on a rockface up at Beithí.
It was sultry heat, we'd been looking for her,
Sweating and panting, driving sheep back
From the cliff-edge when we saw her attacked
On a ledge far down. Crows and more crows
Were eating at her. We heard the cries
But couldn't get near. She was ripped to death
As we suffered her terrible, wild, last breath
And my child's heart broke. I couldn't be calmed
No matter how much she'd tighten her arms
And gather me close. I just cried on
Till she hushed me at last with a piggyback
And the promise of treats of potato-cake.

To-day it's my language that's in its throes,
The poets' passion, my mothers' fathers'
Mothers' language, abandoned and trapped
On a fatal ledge that we won't attempt.
She's in agony, I can hear her heave
And gasp and struggle as they arrive,
The beaked and ravenous scavengers
Who are never far. Oh if only anger
Came howling wild out of her grief,
If only she'd bare the teeth of her love
And rout the pack. But she's giving in,
She's quivering badly, my mother's gone
And promises now won't ease the pain.

translated by Seamus Heaney

NÓTAÍ/*NOTES*

SÉASÚIR/SEASONS

This poem is a free and unrestricted adaptation from the Welsh of Ellis Jones. I first came across a translation of the original in *"The Oxford Book of Welsh Verse in English"*. Later I read a version of the same poem in Ciaran Carson's collection *The New Estate*. My own rendering of the poem is a fortuitous exchange, I hope, between the two sources.

CUMHA NA gCARAD/LAMENT FOR FRIENDSHIP

The idea for this poem is borrowed from the Russian of Yevgeny Yevtushenko. My intermediary was George Reavey whose voluminous edition of *The Poetry of Yevgeny Yevtushenko* was a formative influence. This version was suggested by my reading of *The Sigh* in Reavey's bilingual edition.

ANSEO AG STÁISIÚN CHAISEAL NA gCORR / HERE AT CAISEAL NA gCORR STATION

Once a busy station on the Loch Swilly Railway Line, Caiseal na gCorr is now a gaping windswept ruin alone and abandoned to the silence of the bog. A great vantage point with a sweeping view of the surrounding countryside, Caiseal na gCorr station is a place dear to my heart and to my art.

DO JACK KEROUAC/FOR JACK KEROUAC: (1922 - 1969)

"The strange solitary crazy Catholic mystic" and the inspirational hero of the "beat generation", Kerouac made me a rucksack romantic. *On the Road* became my travelogue for inner-space travel.

SÚILE SHUIBHNE/SWEENEY'S EYES

"Mad Sweeney" the central character in the medieval Gaelic saga *Buile Shuibhne*. He was transformed into a bird-man at the battle of Magh Rath and became a restless and solitary fugitive exiled to the tree-tops, and the mountain slopes.

NA PÍOPAÍ CRÉFÓIGE/CLAY PIPES

Ted Holmes was an American poet who came to live in the vicinity of Falcarragh, sometime in the late sixties. I met him one day while out walking along the backstrand below Falcarragh and we struck up a conversation. He talked a lot about death, about his own deep need to fathom its depth, to understand the "poetry of death." He read aloud a poem by some American contemporary of his. Ted's reading of this poem was very moving. I listened in awe. I was just a youngster and he was the first living poet I had met. This was a momentous occasion for me, a watershed. Years afterwards *'Na Píopaí Créfóige'* arose from my recollection of snatches of Ted's conversation and his reading of that particular poem. Ted Holmes committed suicide in 1972. I hope that he has found his peace *"where the sea meets that moon-blanched land"*.

RÚN BUÍOCHAIS / WORD OF THANKS

And finally I wish to express my sincerest gratitude to Josie Gallagher. His presence gave life to a lot of these poems. I will always remember his friendship, his fortitude and his forthright ways. I wish him well in his wanderings.

Works referred to in the introduction:

The title is a paraphrase from Derick Thomson's poem *Anns a' Bhalbh Mhadainn / Sheep*, taken from *Nua-Bhardachd Gháidhlig / Modern Scottish Gaelic Poems*, Donald Macaulay ed., Southside, Edinburgh 1976. The English translation reads:

> A storm came over my country
> of fine, deadly, smothering snow:
> ... my heart would rejoice
> were I to see on that white plain a yellow spot
> and understand that the breath of the Gael
> > was coming to the surface.

Real People in a Real Place, in *Towards the Human*, Iain Crichton Smith, Macdonald Publishers, Edinburgh 1986.
Mo Bhealach Féin, Seosamh Mac Grianna, Oifig an tSoláthair, Dublin 1940.
Passing the Time: History and Folklore in an Ulster Community, Henry Glasie, O' Brien Press, Dublin 1982.
The excerpt is from the Irish language novel *Bean Ruadh de Dhálach*, Séamas Ó Grianna (Máire), Oifig an tSoláthair, Dublin 1966.
The Donegal Pictures, Rachel Giese, Introduction by Ciaran Carson, Wake Forest University Press, U. S. A., 1987.
Irish Kings and High Kings, Francis John Byrne, Dublin 1973, first paperback edition, B. T. Batsford Ltd, London 1987.
The Dawn is Always New; Selected Poetry of Rocco Scotellaro, Introduction by Dante Della Terza. Princeton University Press, 1980.
An Crann Faoi Bhláth/The Flowering Tree, Declan Kiberd & Gabriel Fitzmaurice, Wolfhound Press, Dublin 1991.

I am indebted to Cathal himself for discussing many of the points in the introduction with me and for helping me to clarify my thinking on them, also to John Logan, Máire Ní Neachtain and Róisín Ní Néill who carefully read the script and who made many valuable suggestions.